Macmillan McGraw-Hill

Math Connects
4

Reteach and Skills Practice Workbook

Macmillan/McGraw-Hill

TO THE STUDENT   This *Reteach and Skills Practice Workbook* gives you additional examples and problems for the concept exercises in each lesson. The exercises are designed to help you study mathematics by reinforcing important skills needed to succeed in the everyday world. The materials are organized by chapter and lesson, with one Reteach and one Skills Practice worksheet for every lesson in *Math Connects, Grade 3*.

Always keep your workbook handy. Along with you textbook, daily homework, and class notes, the completed *Reteach and Skills Practice Workbook* can help you in reviewing for quizzes and tests.

TO THE TEACHER   These worksheets are the same ones found in the Chapter Resource Masters for *Math Connects, Grade 3*. The answers to these worksheets are available at the end of each Chapter Resource Masters booklet.

The *McGraw·Hill* Companies

 Macmillan/McGraw-Hill

Send all inquiries to:
Macmillan/McGraw-Hill
8787 Orion Place
Columbus, OH 43240

ISBN: 978-0-02-107305-4
MHID: 0-02-107305-8   *Reteach and Skills Practice Workbook, Grade 4*

Printed in the United States of America.

7 8 9 10 HES 14 13 12 11 10

CONTENTS

Name _____

Reteach

Place Value Through Hundred Thousands

You can write numbers in different ways using words and digits. The place value chart below shows the value of each digit in the number 237,568. Below the chart, the number appears in standard form, word form, and expanded form.

Thousands Period			Ones Period		
hundreds	tens	ones	hundreds	tens	ones
2	3	7	5	6	8

Standard form Uses digits: 237,568

Word form Uses words to write the number the way you say it:
Two hundred thirty-seven thousand, five hundred sixty-eight.

Expanded form Uses the place value of each digit to write the number: 200,000 + 30,000 + 7,000 + 500 + 60 + 8

Complete the expanded form of each number below.

1. $87,562 = 80,000 +$ _____ $+ 500 +$ _____ $+ 2$

2. $431,281 = 400,000 +$ _____ $+ 1,000 +$
   _____ $+ 80 +$ ___

Complete the chart by filling in the standard form and word form of each number:

Standard Form	Expanded Form	Word Form
3._____	100,000 + 20,000 + 600 + 40 + 9	_____
4._____	300,000 + 30,000 + 8,000 + 200 + 30 + 7	_____
5._____	500,000 + 10,000 + 3,000 + 400 + 60 + 1	_____

Name _____

Skills Practice

Place Value Through Hundred Thousands

Write each number in standard form.

1. five hundred eighty-two thousand, nine hundred forty-seven.

   _____

2. two hundred six thousand, four hundred twenty-nine.

   _____

3. eight hundred thirty-four thousand, six hundred seventy-one.

   _____

Write each number in word form and expanded form.

4. 6,829

   _____

   _____

5. 23,741

   _____

   _____

6. 119,874

   _____

   _____

   _____

7. 745,293

   _____

   _____

   _____

Complete the expanded form.

8. $37,568 = 30,000 + \underline{\hspace{2cm}} + 500 + \underline{\hspace{1.5cm}} + 8$

9. $493,236 = 400,000 + \underline{\hspace{2cm}} + 3,000 + \underline{\hspace{1cm}} + 30 + \underline{\hspace{0.8cm}}$

10. $548,912 = 500,000 + \underline{\hspace{2cm}} + 8,000 + 900 + \underline{\hspace{1cm}} + 2$

1-2

Reteach

Place Value Through Millions

Numbers can be written in different ways using words or digits. The place value chart below shows the value of each digit in the number 14,153,987. Below the chart, the number appears in standard form, word form, and expanded form.

Millions Period			Thousands Period			Ones Period		
hundreds	tens	ones	hundreds	tens	ones	hundreds	tens	ones
	1	4	1	5	3	9	8	7

Standard form Uses digits to write a number: 14,153,987

Word form Uses words to write a number the way you say it: Fourteen million, one hundred fifty-three thousand, nine hundred eighty-seven

Expanded form Uses the place value of each digit to write the

number: 10,000,000 + 4,000,000 + 100,000 + 50,000 + 3,000 +

900 + 80 + 7

Complete the chart.

Standard Form	Expanded Form	Word Form
1._____	7,000,000 + 300,000 + 50,000 + 6,000 + 200 + 30 + 7	_____ _____
2._____	40,000,000 + 1,000,000 + 600,000 + 50,000 + 9,000 + 700 + 3	_____ _____
3._____	200,000,000 + 30,000,000 + 5,000,000 + 90,000 + 1,000 + 500 + 60 + 8	_____ _____

Name _____

Skills Practice

Place Value Through Millions

Write each number in standard form.

1. four million, nine hundred twenty-seven thousand, two hundred
   fifteen _____

2. ninety-seven million, two hundred fifty-three thousand, eight
   hundred twenty-five _____

Write each number in word form and expanded form.

3. 275,364,819

   _____

   _____

   _____

   _____

4. 843,720,159

   _____

   _____

   _____

   _____

Complete the expanded form.

5. $413,089,762 = 400,000,000 +$ _____ $+ 3,000,000 +$
   $80,000 +$ _____ $+ 700 +$ _____ $+ 2$

6. $152,387,093 = 100,000,000 +$ _____ $+ 2,000,000 +$
   $300,000 +$ _____ $+ 7,000 +$ _____ $+ 3$

7. $9,262,548 = 9,000,000 +$ _____ $+ 60,000 +$
   $2,000 +$ _____ $+ 40 +$ _____

Write the value of the underlined digit.

8. 1,2<u>8</u>3,479 _____   9. 50,<u>9</u>07,652 _____

10. 20,<u>7</u>35,823 _____   11. <u>3</u>18,472,008 _____

1-3

Reteach

Problem-Solving Strategy: The Four-Step Plan

The Four-Step Plan

If you want to solve a problem, it is important to have a plan. You can use the four-step plan to solve most problems. Use this exercise to learn more:

Miguel's class is having a picnic. The class will make sandwiches at the picnic. There are 36 students in Miguel's class and 18 slices of bread in a loaf. How many loaves of bread will Miguel's class need for the picnic? (*Hint:* Each sandwich will have 2 slices of bread.)

Step 1

Understand What facts do you know? Miguel's class has 36 students. There are 18 slices of bread in one loaf. What do you need to find? How many loaves of bread the class will need for the picnic.

Step 2

Plan You can multiply the number of sandwiches needed by the number of slices of bread needed for each sandwich. Then divide the total number of slices by the number of slices in a loaf.

Step 3

Solve 36 sandwiches $\times$ 2 slices of bread for each sandwich = 72 slices of bread. Then divide 72 slices of bread by 18 slices in a loaf: $\frac{72}{18} = 4$. So, Miguel's class will need 4 loaves of bread to make sandwiches for everyone at the picnic.

Step 4

Check Look back at the problem. One way to check the answer to this problem is to work backwards. How many slices of bread are in 4 loaves? $4 \times 18 = 72$. How many sandwiches does 72 slices of bread make? $\frac{72}{2} = 36$. So the answer is correct.

Reteach   (continued)

Problem-Solving Strategy: The Four-Step Plan

Solve. Use the four-step plan.

1. Sarah's school has 280 students who want to play in a basketball tournament. The tournament needs to have 1 game ball for every two teams. If each team will have 5 players, how many basketballs will the tournament need?

   _____

   _____

2. Josh and Anthony have a lemonade stand. They sell 2 glasses of lemonade for $1. They sell 14 glasses each afternoon. How much money do Josh and Anthony make after 3 days of selling lemonade?

   _____

   _____

3. Jessica can ride her bike 3 blocks in 1 minute. It takes her twice as long to ride her bike 3 blocks if she carries her backpack. If her school is 12 blocks from her house, how long will it take her to get to school with a full backpack?

   _____

   _____

4. A group of friends needs to carry a large basket of books to the library. Kevin can carry the basket 5 feet. Rachel can carry it 3 feet farther than Kevin. Daniel can carry the basket half as far as Rachel. If each friend carries the basket 3 times, how far will they move the basket?

   _____

   _____

Name _____

Skills Practice

Problem-Solving Strategy

Solve. Use the four-step plan.

1. Javier's grandmother lives 120 miles away. It takes 1 hour to go 40 miles by train. How long will it take for Javier to get to his grandmother's home by train?

   _____

2. The average fourth-grader at Jones Elementary School can complete 2 math problems in 1 minute. A teacher assigned 24 math problems for homework. How long will it take for each student to complete the homework?

   _____

3. Brittany wants to make cookies for the whole fourth grade. Her recipe makes 1 dozen cookies. There are 72 fourth-graders at her school. How many dozens of cookies does Brittany need to make for the whole grade?

   _____

4. Justin is paid $2 a week for doing chores around the house. He wants to buy a new football that costs $12. How many weeks will Justin have to save his money to buy the football?

   _____

5. Last year 485,675 fans came to see the Fantastics play. This year 457,382 fans came. How many fewer fans came to see the Fantastics this year?

   _____

6. In 2000, about 4,508,345 people lived in Jefferson County. Experts predict that 5,763,123 people will live there in 2010. How many more people will live in Jefferson County in 2010?

   _____

1-4

Reteach

Compare Whole Numbers

You compare numbers when you want to know if one number is **less than**, **greater than**, or **equal to** another number. You can use a number line or a place value chart to help you compare numbers. Compare **12,572** and **15,572**.

Lesser numbers are on the left on a number line. Greater numbers are on the right.

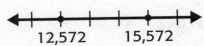

12,572 is to the left of 15,572. So 12,572 ◯ 15,572.

In a place value chart, you start at the left. Look for the first place where the digits are different to compare the numbers.

Thousands Period			Ones Period		
hundreds	tens	ones	hundreds	tens	ones
	1	2	5	7	2
	1	5	5	7	2
	same	different	same	same	same

The number 15,572 has more thousands than 12,572.

So 15,572 ◯ 12,572.

Compare. Use >, <, or =.

1. 42,615 ◯ 42,637

2. 13,982 ◯ 13,874

3. 4,765 ◯ 4,219

4. 8,097 ◯ 8,790

5. 7,123 ◯ 7,186

6. 5,835 ◯ 5,083

7. 11,093 ◯ 10,930

8. 13,771 ◯ 13,781

9. 65,987 ◯ 65,987

10. 81,092 ◯ 81,902

11. 124,764 ◯ 124,674

12. 245,718 ◯ 247,518

13. 718,634 ◯ 719,055

14. 3,870,762 ◯ 3,780,763

Name _____

Skills Practice

Compare Whole Numbers

Compare. Use >, <, or =.

1. 1,276 ◯ 1,267

2. 1,589 ◯ 1,587

3. 2,235 ◯ 2,325

4. 4,672 ◯ 4,670

5. 8,902 ◯ 8,912

6. 10,321 ◯ 10,231

7. 14,832 ◯ 14,872

8. 38,087 ◯ 37,088

9. 67,982 ◯ 67,892

10. 100,542 ◯ 105,042

11. 165,982 ◯ 178,983

12. 239,742 ◯ 289,650

13. 563,218 ◯ 652,985

14. 1,986,034 ◯ 1,896,075

15. two hundred fifty-two thousand, nine hundred eighty-five

   ◯ 252,895

16. 300,000 + 60,000 + 2,000 + 300 + 10 + 7 ◯ 364,375

17. five hundred thousand, nine hundred twenty-seven

   ◯ 500,000 + 900 + 20 + 7

18. 621,743 ◯ six hundred twenty thousand, seven hundred fifty-nine

19. 14,210,312 ◯ forty million, two hundred thousand, seventy-five

Solve.

20. Jorge has 1,325 baseball cards in his collection. Sam wants to have more cards than Jorge by the end of summer. Sam collects 1,297 cards. Who has more cards?

   _____

21. Andrea wants to live in the city with the most people. She read that New York City has 8,008,278 people and that Seoul, South Korea has 10,231,217 people. Where does Andrea want to live?

   _____

Name _____

Reteach

Order Whole Numbers

Order the numbers from greatest to least: 9,245; 6,082; 8,970; 5,329.
You can use a number line or a place value chart to help you order
numbers.

Once you place the numbers where they belong on a number line, you
can see their order.

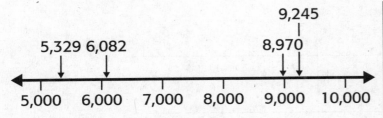

| 9,245 is farthest to the right. It is the greatest number.
5,329 is the farthest to the left. It is the least number. |

In a place value chart, you start at the left. Look for the first place
where the digits are different to compare the numbers. Continue
through each place value until you have ordered all the numbers.

Thousands Period			Ones Period		
hundreds	tens	ones	hundreds	tens	ones
		9 (greatest),	2	4	5
		6 (third),	0	8	2
		8 (second),	9	7	0
		5 (least),	3	2	9

The number 9,245 has more thousands than all the other numbers. It
is the greatest. 5,329 has the least thousands, so it is the least.

Order the numbers from greatest to least.

1. 1,287; 1,509; 1,487; 1,111

   _____

2. 4,278; 5,761; 4,390; 5,104

   _____

3. 7,861; 10,865; 9,200; 8,923

   _____

Name _____

Skills Practice

Order Whole Numbers

Order the numbers from greatest to least.

1. 1,209; 1,078; 1,165; 1,318

_____

2. 5,982; 6,237; 7,892; 4,163

_____

3. 27,982; 32,563; 34,138; 29,238

_____

4. 65,201; 64,827; 66,482; 63,621

_____

Order the numbers from least to greatest.

5. 8,362; 8,435; 8,920; 8,231

_____

6. 38,271; 37,462; 30,256; 34,247

_____

7. 278,623; 265,023; 281,426; 252,917

_____

8. 4,293,046; 4,308,261; 4,287,460; 4,260,658

_____

9. 57,294,601; 58,925,462; 55,281,473; 56,024,482

_____

Solve.

10. The all-county track meet was Friday. Below are the times for the fastest
    1-mile runs. The coaches need help figuring out who gets the second
    place ribbon. Order these race times from least to greatest.

    Brianna: 362 seconds   Lauren: 365 seconds
    Rachel: 358 seconds   Danielle: 370 seconds

    Whose time was the second least in seconds?

_____

1-6

Reteach

Round Whole Numbers

Round the number 14,682 to the nearest hundred.

A number line helps you round by showing you which number is closer to the number you are rounding. 14,682 is between 14,600 and 14,700. It is closer to 14,700. You round to 14,700.

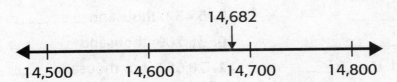

Place value helps you round by showing you which digit to round.

Thousands Period			Ones Period		
hundreds	tens	ones	hundreds	tens	ones
	1	4 ,	6	8	2

↑ 10,000   ↑ 4,000   ↑ 600   ↑ 80   ↑ 2

- Find place value to be rounded. (hundreds)
- Look at digit to the right of the place you are rounding. (tens)
- Round up, or add 1 to the place you are rounding, if the digit to the right is 5 or greater. Round down, or add 0 to the place you are rounding, if the digit is less than 5. (digit is 8; round up)
- Replace all digits after the place you are rounding with zeros. (14,700)

Round each number to the given place-value position.

1. 657; hundred _____

2. 843; hundred _____

3. 2,190; thousand _____

4. 7,841; thousand _____

5. 15,834; ten thousand _____

6. 33,512; ten thousand _____

7. 243,713; hundred thousand _____

8. 687,351; hundred thousand _____

9. 537,820; ten thousand _____

10. 274,871; ten thousand _____

11. 2,763,640; million _____

12. 6,380,639; million _____

Name _____

Skills Practice

Round Whole Numbers

Round each number to the given place-value position.

1. 482; ten _____   2. 747; ten _____

3. 261; hundred _____   4. 375; hundred _____

5. 1,278; hundred _____   6. 3,568; hundred _____

7. 4,763; thousand _____   8. 5,432; thousand _____

9. 12,854; thousand _____   10. 35,709; thousand _____

11. 42,981; ten thousand _____   12. 78,651; ten thousand _____

13. 267,430; hundred thousand _____   14. 449,843; hundred thousand _____

15. 1,652,804; hundred thousand _____

16. 2,398,526; hundred thousand _____

17. 4,875,062; million _____

18. 12,392,604; million _____

Solve.

19. The Environmental Protection Agency says the Mississippi River is 2,320 miles long. The U.S. Geological Survey says it is 2,300 miles long. Rounded to the nearest hundred, are these two numbers about the same? Explain. _____

_____

20. The state of California has a land area of 163,692 square miles. Montana has a land area of 147,042 square miles. Rounded to the nearest ten thousand, are the two states' areas the same? Explain.

_____

_____

21. Rounding to the hundreds place, Devin has to score about 200 points to make the traveling basketball team. He has scored 135 points so far. How many more points will he need to score to make the team? Explain. _____

_____

Name _____

Reteach

Problem-Solving Investigation: Choose a Strategy

Sometimes you can solve a problem using more than one strategy.
You must choose the strategy that works best for you.

Use this problem to learn more about choosing a strategy:

Sam has 3 shirts to give to his friends. Each friend has one favorite color
that is either red, blue, or green. Michelle does not like red or green.
Ben does not like blue or red. Lindsey likes red. Who likes green?

Understand	You know there are three friends: Michelle, Ben, and Lindsey. You know there are three shirts: red, blue, and green. You need to find out who likes green.
Plan	Choose a strategy. You have information about three people, but some information is missing for each person. A table is a good way to show what information you have and what information is missing. Make a table to solve the problem.
Solve	<table><tr><td></td><td>**Red**</td><td>**Blue**</td><td>**Green**</td></tr><tr><td>**Michelle**</td><td>**No**</td><td>yes</td><td>**No**</td></tr><tr><td>**Ben**</td><td>**No**</td><td>**No**</td><td>yes</td></tr><tr><td>**Lindsey**</td><td>**Yes**</td><td>no</td><td>no</td></tr></table> Since each friend has only one favorite color, you can fill in the rest of the information for each friend. Ben is the friend who likes green.
Check	Look back at the problem. Does the chart show one favorite color for each friend? _____ yes

Name _____

Reteach (continued)

Problem-Solving Investigation

Use any strategy shown below to solve. Tell which one you used.

- Use the four-step plan
- Draw a picture
- Look for a pattern
- Make a table

1. Alejandro collected bugs for a science project. He has a painted lady butterfly, a monarch butterfly, a bumble bee, a lime butterfly, a honey bee, a speckled wood butterfly, a carpenter bee, and a plum Judy butterfly. Did he collect more bees or butterflies?

   _____

   _____

   _____

2. Isaiah is growing his dog-walking business. The first week he walked 1 dog. The second week he walked 2 dogs. The third week he walked 3 dogs. If this pattern continues, how many dogs will Isaiah walk the seventh week?

   _____

   _____

   _____

3. Carlos lives 2 blocks west of Kimberly. Elizabeth lives 2 blocks east of Kimberly. How far does Elizabeth live from Carlos?

   _____

   _____

   _____

4. Kelly earns $5 every time she washes her neighbor's car. How many times will she need to wash the car to earn $45?

   _____

   _____

   _____

1-7

Skills Practice

Problem-Solving Investigation: Choose a Strategy

Use any strategy shown below to solve. Tell which one you used.

- Use the four-step plan
- Draw a picture
- Look for a pattern
- Make a table

1. A cheetah can run 70 miles in one hour. A rabbit can run 35 miles in one hour. How many hours would it take a rabbit to run as far as a cheetah can run in 2 hours?

_____

2. Mrs. Jones said the class could decide what game they played this afternoon. The class listed these games: four square, basketball, kickball, four square, kickball, soccer, four square, basketball, four square. Which game should the class play?

_____

3. Cameron says he runs about 4 miles when he plays a soccer game. Last week he ran about 12 miles. How many soccer games did he play?

_____

4. The zoo is 5 miles from Katie's house. Her school is 2 miles farther. Katie's grandmother lives another 3 miles past her school. How far away is Katie's grandmother's house from Katie's house?

_____

5. Courtney can make 5 bracelets a week. She wants to make one for each girl in her class. If there are 17 girls in her class, how many weeks will it take her to make the bracelets?

_____

6. Zack has 4 younger brothers. Zack is 54 inches tall. The next oldest, James, is 52 inches tall. The next oldest, Kyle, is 50 inches tall. The next oldest, Thomas, is 48 inches tall. How tall is the youngest brother, Andrew?

_____

Name _____

Reteach

Algebra: Addition Properties and Subtraction Rules

We use addition properties and subtraction rules to add and subtract. These properties and rules help us add numbers mentally. There are three main properties of addition and two subtraction rules to keep in mind as you add and subtract.

Addition Properties

Commutative Property	Associative Property	Identity Property
The order in which numbers are added does not change the sum.	The way in which numbers are grouped when added does not change the sum.	The sum of any number and 0 is the number.
Example $3 + 1 = 4$ $1 + 3 = 4$	**Example** $(6 + 5) + 2 \quad 6 + (5 + 2)$ $11 + 2 \quad 6 + 7$ $13 \qquad 13$	**Example** $9 + 0 = 9$ $0 + 9 = 9$

Subtraction Rules

When you subtract 0 from any number, the result is the number. **Examples** $7 - 0 = 7 \quad 5 - 0 = 5$	When you subtract any number from itself, the result is 0. **Examples** $8 - 8 = 0 \quad 4 - 4 = 0$

Complete each number sentence. Identify the property or rule used.

1. $5 + (3 + 4) = (3 + 4) + \square$ _____

2. $\square + 0 = 7$ _____

3. $6 - \square = 0$ _____

4. $2 - \square = 2$ _____

5. $(3 + 2) + 5 = 3 + (2 + \square)$ _____

Name _____

Skills Practice

Algebra: Addition Properties and Subtraction Rules

Complete each number sentence. Identify the property or rule used.

1. $(89 + 54) + 23 = 89 + (54 + \underline{\hspace{1cm}})$ _____

2. $\underline{\hspace{1cm}} + 0 = 357$ _____

3. $(36 + 14) + \underline{\hspace{1cm}} = (14 + 36) + 9$ _____

4. $693 + \underline{\hspace{1cm}} = 693$ _____

5. $(7 + 19) + 3 = \underline{\hspace{1cm}} + (19 + 3)$ _____

6. $678 + 0 = \underline{\hspace{1cm}}$ _____

7. $69 - \underline{\hspace{1cm}} = 0$ _____

8. $36 + (128 + 10) = (\underline{\hspace{1cm}} + 10) + 36$ _____

9. $\underline{\hspace{1cm}} + 0 = 58$ _____

10. $987 + \underline{\hspace{1cm}} = 452 + 987$ _____

11. $79 - \underline{\hspace{1cm}} = 79$ _____

12. $(8 + 32) + \underline{\hspace{1cm}} = 8 + (32 + 4)$ _____

2-2

Reteach

Estimate Sums and Differences

When the word "about" is used in a problem, you should find an estimate. An estimate is an answer close to the exact answer. When estimating, you can round to the nearest ten, hundred, thousand, or ten thousand.

Estimate: 1,262 + 639.

Round to the   1,262 + 639
nearest hundreds   ↓   ↓
place. Then add.

               1,300 + 600 = 1,900

So, 1,262 + 639 is about 1,900.

Estimate: 798 − 246.

Round to the   798 − 246
nearest tens place.   ↓   ↓
Then subtract.

             800 − 250 − 550.

So, 798 − 246 is about 550.

Estimate. Round to the indicated place value.

1. 277 + 439; ten _____

2. 3,857 − 899; hundred _____

3. 1,295 − 735; hundred _____

4. 689 − 640; ten _____

5. 25,633 + 33,821; thousand _____

6. 574 + 888; hundred _____

7. 15,529 − 13,178; thousand _____

8. 11,827 + 10,431; thousand _____

9. 32,441 + 12,532; thousand _____

10. 1,348 + 1,498; hundred _____

11. 88,188 − 15,644; thousand _____

12. 52,661 − 31,822; thousand _____

Name _____

Skills Practice

Estimate Sums and Differences

Round to the nearest ten.

1. 613
   + 187   _____

2. $783
   + $321   _____

3. 891
   − 134   _____

4. 591
   − 214   _____

Round to the nearest hundred.

5. $763
   + $271   _____

6. 824
   + 668   _____

7. 4,719
   +3,261   _____

8. 8,635
   − 5,478   _____

9. 14,597
   − 7,346   _____

10. $26,783
    − $13,539   _____

Round to the nearest thousand.

11. 33,261
    +48,945   _____

12. 57,698
    + 21,812   _____

13. $77,418
    − $53,599   _____

14. 84,524
    − 62,701   _____

15. In 1787 Delaware became the first state of the United States.
    About how many years ago did Delaware become a state?

    _____

2-3

Reteach

Problem-Solving Skill: Estimate or Exact Answer

You **estimate** an answer when you do not need an exact answer.
Find an **exact** answer when you need to find *exactly* how much.

Logan's neighbor hires him to mow his lawn. Logan charges $6.25 an hour to mow a yard. The neighbor asks Logan how much it will cost to mow his yard. Logan thinks it will take about 2 hours to mow his lawn. How much does Logan tell his neighbor it will cost?

Understand

What facts do you know?

- Logan charges $6.25 an hour
- It will take Logan about 2 hours to mow

What do you need to find?

How much it will cost Logan's neighbor to have his lawn mowed.

Plan

Does Logan need an exact answer or an estimate?

Is his neighbor expecting an estimate or exact answer?

> Logan will only be able to give an estimate for the cost because there is no way for him to know *exactly* how long it will take to mow the yard. His neighbor should expect an estimate.

Solve

How much does Logan charge if it takes him 2 hours?

$6.25 + $6.25 = $12.50

Check

When determining how long it will take to mow the lawn, is it better for Logan to estimate higher or lower? Explain.

> It is better for Logan to estimate higher. A higher estimate will prevent Logan from charging his neighbor much more than the original estimated cost.

Name _____

Reteach

Problem-Solving Skills   (continued)

**Tell whether an estimate or an exact answer is needed.
Then solve.**

1. Marcus, Jon, and Brenda all collect fossils. Marcus has 13 fossils, Jon has 28 fossils, and Brenda has 17 fossils. Do they have more than 70 fossils in all?

    _____

2. Ramona went to the store to purchase some apples. The apples cost $3.75, and she gives the cashier a $10 bill. About how much

    change should Ramona get back? _____

3. Raphael needs enough hose to reach his garden, which is 20 feet away from the water spout. He has one section of hose that is 14 feet long and another section that is 7 feet long. Will the hose be long enough if he connects the two sections?

    _____

4. Ms. Ramirez wants her students to each have one muffin. She has 27 students in her class. If each box of muffins contains 10, how many boxes will she need?

    _____

5. Julie has $20. She wants to buy a box of cereal for $4, a game for $6, and a pair of mittens for $8. Will she have enough money for

    her purchases? _____

6. Gerald is reading a novel. On Monday he reads 37 pages, on Tuesday he reads 24 pages, and on Wednesday he reads 26 pages. About how many pages has Gerald read?

    _____

7. Matthew has two buckets. One of his buckets holds 78 ounces of water, and his other bucket holds 95 ounces of water. If Matthew fills his buckets all the way, exactly how much water can he carry?

    _____

2-3

Skills Practice

Problem-Solving Skill: Estimate or Exact Answer

**Tell whether an estimate or an exact answer is needed.
Then solve.**

1. A family drove 184 miles to visit friends and then drove 213 miles to the beach. About how many miles did they drive?

_____

2. A zoo has 2 hippopotamuses that each eats 120 pounds of grass a day. Is 370 pounds of grass enough to feed them for 2 days?

_____

3. While on vacation, Isabel took 124 pictures, Jacob took 96 pictures and Maya took 178 pictures. About how many pictures did they all take?

_____

4. Brian scored a 72 on his first science quiz. On his second science quiz, Brian scored a 98. By about how many points did Brian improve his score?

_____

5. Travis ran the 50-yard dash in 10.47 seconds. After practicing, Travis ran the 50-yard dash in 8.32 seconds. About how many seconds faster was Travis after practicing?

_____

6. Maria is shopping for school clothes. She buys a sweater for $29, a jacket for $41, and a skirt for $18. How much money does she spend?

_____

2-4

Reteach

Add Whole Numbers

The traditional method of adding whole numbers is from right to left. Did you know whole numbers can also be added from left to right?

Adding from left to right is a good method to try when adding in your head.

Find 358 + 968.	$\begin{array}{r} 358 \\ + 968 \end{array}$
Step 1: Add the hundreds. $\begin{array}{r} 300 \\ + 900 \\ \hline 1,200 \end{array}$	**Step 2:** Add the tens. $\begin{array}{r} 50 \\ + 60 \\ \hline 110 \end{array}$
Step 3: Add the ones. $\begin{array}{r} 8 \\ + 8 \\ \hline 16 \end{array}$	**Step 4:** Add the answers. $\begin{array}{r} 1,200 \\ 110 \\ + \quad 16 \\ \hline 1,326 \end{array}$

Find each sum. Check your work by estimating.

1. $\begin{array}{r} 574 \\ + 361 \end{array}$ _____

2. $\begin{array}{r} 1,361 \\ + \quad 627 \end{array}$ _____

3. $\begin{array}{r} 3,254 \\ + 4,563 \end{array}$ _____

4. $\begin{array}{r} 477 \\ + 534 \end{array}$ _____

5. $\begin{array}{r} 2,225 \\ + \quad 384 \end{array}$ _____

6. $\begin{array}{r} 5,821 \\ + 7,338 \end{array}$ _____

7. $\begin{array}{r} 328 \\ + 492 \end{array}$ _____

8. $\begin{array}{r} 6,578 \\ + \quad 679 \end{array}$ _____

9. $\begin{array}{r} 8,634 \\ + 3,766 \end{array}$ _____

10. $\begin{array}{r} 853 \\ + 625 \end{array}$ _____

11. $\begin{array}{r} 4,135 \\ + \quad 681 \end{array}$ _____

12. $\begin{array}{r} 7,254 \\ 8,563 \\ + 2,188 \end{array}$ _____

Name _____

Skills Practice

Add Whole Numbers

Find each sum. Check your work by estimating.

1. 297
  + 608

2. 864
  + 391

3. $5,203
  + $ 739

4. 2,989
  + 4,571

5. 27,429
  + 7,302

6. $45,209
  + $31,854

7. 67,813
  + 24,976

8. 40,287
  + 89,153

9. $n = \$603 + \$237$ _____

10. $\$37 + \$7 = n$ _____

11. $57,153 + 12,899 = n$ _____

12. $n = 5,897 + 1,379$ _____

The table shows the size of various states in square miles.

State	Total area in square miles
Alaska	656,425
California	163,707
Maine	35,387
New Jersey	8,722
North Dakota	70,704
Texas	268,601

13. What is the combined area of the two largest states?

_____

Name _____

Reteach

Subtract Whole Numbers

Subtraction of whole numbers is similar to addition of whole numbers in that you may need to regroup.

Find 481 — 292.	481 — 292
Step 1: Rewrite the problem.	4 hundreds 8 tens 1 one — 2 hundreds 9 tens 2 ones
Step 2: Regroup 1 of the hundreds into an equivalent 10 tens.	3 hundreds 18 tens 1 one — 2 hundreds 9 tens 2 ones
Step 3: Regroup 1 of the tens into an equivalent 10 ones.	3 hundreds 17 tens 11 ones — 2 hundreds 9 tens 2 ones
Step 4: Subtract. 481 — 292 = 189	3 hundreds 17 tens 11 ones — 2 hundreds 9 tens 2 ones 1 hundreds 8 tens 9 ones

Subtract. Use addition or estimation to check.

1.   561
  − 272

2.   811
  − 428

3.   785
  − 494

4.   1,261
  − 633

5.   2,536
  − 844

6.   8,831
  − 566

7.   5,619
  − 2,828

8.   9,116
  − 5,853

9.   2,914
  − 1,265

Name _____

Skills Practice

Subtract Whole Numbers

Subtract. Use addition or estimation to check.

1. 491
   − 247

2. 7,548
   − 3,657

3. $661
   −$275

4. 631
   − 418

5. 613
   − 174

6. 71,327
   − 34,589

7. $6,169 - 1,578 = n$ _____

8. $\$351 - \$282 = n$ _____

9. $n = \$913 - \$268$ _____

10. $n = 536,319 - 478,258$ _____

This table shows the dates of significant American conflicts.

	Began	Ended
Revolutionary War	1775	1783
War of 1812	1812	1815
Civil War	1861	1865
World War I	1914	1918
World War II	1939	1945
Vietnam War	1954	1975

11. How many years after the Revolutionary War ended did the Civil War begin? _____

12. How long did the Vietnam War last? _____

Reteach

Problem-Solving Investigation: Choose a Strategy

Sally has 305 stickers, Joan has 403 stickers, and Karen has 377 stickers. Do the girls have more than 1,000 stickers altogether?

Organize your information using the four-step plan. Then solve.

Understand

What facts do you know?

- Sally has 305 stickers.
- Joan has 403 stickers.
- Karen has 377 stickers.

What do you need to know?
About how many stickers the girls have altogether.

Plan

We do not need an exact answer so we can use estimation to solve the problem.

Solve

Round each number then add to find about how many altogether.

$305 \longrightarrow \quad 300$
$403 \longrightarrow \quad 400$
$377 \longrightarrow \quad \underline{+\ 400}$
$\qquad\qquad\quad 1,100$

We rounded up one time so our estimate is high.
Since 377 is 23 less than 400, our estimate will be close.
So, the girls will have more than 1,000 stickers.

Check

To check we can subtract or numbers to check our calculations.

$1,100 - 400 = 700$
$700 - 400 = 300$
$300 - 300 = 0$

So, our estimate was correct.

Name _____

Reteach

Problem-Solving Investigation   (continued)

Use the four-step plan, estimation, or an exact answer to solve.

1. Paco has 129 toy cars. His brother has 167 toy cars. How many toy cars do they have in all? _____

2. Hatori has 429 football cards, 278 baseball cards, and 97 hockey cards. Does Hatori have more than 1,000 cards in all? Explain.

   _____

3. The school cafeteria is ordering napkins. Each package has 500 napkins. Every day at least 200 napkins are used. How many packeges will the cafeteria need to order for 2 weeks?

   _____

4. Mrs. Potter went to the grocery store. She bought 15 cans of soup. Her family eats soup twice a week. How long will the soup last?

   _____

5. The store sells 150 bottles of water each week. The bottles come in packages of 25. The store ordered 5 packages. Do they have enough for the week? Explain. _____

For exercises 6–7 use the menu below to solve.

Lunch Menu	
Item	**Price**
Peanut Butter Sandwich	$2
Soup of the Day	$3
Baked Potato	$2
Water	$1
Juice	$1
Milk	50¢

6. Jeremy has $6 he can spend on lunch. If he buys soup, a sandwich, and juice will he have enough to buy anything else? Explain. _____

7. Nika wants to buy a baked potato and milk. How much will she need in all? _____

2-6

Skills Practice

Problem-Solving Investigation: Choose a Strategy

Use the four-step plan, estimation, or an exact answer to solve each problem.

1. James, Max, and Melba collect baseball cards. James has 870 cards, Max has 569 cards, and Melba has 812 cards. Do the three friends have more than 2,000 baseball cards? Explain.

   _____

   _____

2. Nicki has a collection of 79 shells and 64 rocks. How many items are in her collection? Explain.

   _____

   _____

3. Kelly has a coin collection. Her quarters are worth $104. Her dimes are worth $75. Her nickels are worth $27. What is the total value of Kelly's coin collection?

   _____

4. The Comic Book Show sells 474 tickets on Friday and 396 tickets on Saturday. About how many tickets does the Comic Book Show sell? Explain.

   _____

   _____

   _____

5. How many people visited the museum on Saturday and Sunday?

   _____

6. About how many people visited the museum on Wednesday, Thursday, and Friday?

   _____

Museum Visitors	
Wednesday	377
Thursday	405
Friday	529
Saturday	836
Sunday	915

Name _____

Reteach

Subtract Across Zeros

Subtraction that involves digits that are zero has the same steps as subtraction that involves digits that are not zero.

Find 300−157.	$\begin{array}{r} 300 \\ -\ 157 \\ \hline \end{array}$
Step 1: Regroup the hundreds by converting 1 hundred into 10 tens.	$\begin{array}{r} {}^{2}\!\!\not{3}\,{}^{10}\!\!\not{0}\,0 \\ -\ 1\ 5\ 7 \\ \hline \end{array}$
Step 2: Regroup the tens by converting 1 ten into 10 ones.	$\begin{array}{r} {}^{9} \\ 2\ {}^{1}\!\!\not{0}\,10 \\ \not{3}\ \not{0}\ \not{0} \\ -\ 1\ 5\ 7 \\ \hline \end{array}$
Step 3: Subtract.	$\begin{array}{r} {}^{9} \\ 2\ {}^{1}\!\!\not{0}\,10 \\ \not{3}\ \not{0}\ \not{0} \\ -\ 1\ 5\ 7 \\ \hline 1\ 4\ 3 \end{array}$

Subtract. Use addition to check.

1. $\begin{array}{r} 400 \\ -\ 158 \\ \hline \end{array}$

2. $\begin{array}{r} 3,900 \\ -\ 1,853 \\ \hline \end{array}$

3. $\begin{array}{r} \$800 \\ -\ \$267 \\ \hline \end{array}$

4. $\begin{array}{r} 6,000 \\ -\ 4,322 \\ \hline \end{array}$

5. $\begin{array}{r} 600 \\ -\ 319 \\ \hline \end{array}$

6. $\begin{array}{r} 9,000 \\ -\ 6,866 \\ \hline \end{array}$

Name _____

Skills Practice

Subtract Across Zeros

Subtract. Use addition to check.

1. 700
   − 280

2. 9,000
   − 3,512

3. 500
   − 361

4. $8,000
   − $2,987

5. 900
   −722

6. 5,000
   − 3,159

7. 300
   − 143

8. $6,800 − $4,211 = n _____

9. 4,100
   − 2,487

10. 8,000 − 2,533 = n _____

Complete the following tables using the rules.

11.

Rule: Subtract 356		
Input	2,200	_____
Output	_____	2,844

12.

Rule: Subtract 1,125		
Input	8,000	_____
Output	_____	8,875

3-1

Reteach

Collect and Organize Data

Marcia counted the number of letters in each word in a story. The data is shown below.

Number of Letters in Words in a Story

3	3	5	6	4	2	1	5	6	3	4	7
3	2	3	5	2	8	4	5	3	3	5	2
5	6	3	5	1	4						

You can **organize** the data in a tally chart or a frequency table.

Example: For the first number, 3, make a tally mark in the table. Cross out the 3 in the data above. Then record and cross out the remaining 3s. In the frequency table record the number of occurrences you recorded in the tally chart.

Complete the tally chart and the frequency table.

Number of Letters in Words in a Story		
Number of Letters in Words	Tally	
1	||	
2		
3	﹢﹢﹢﹢ |||	
4		
5		
6		
7		
8		

Number of Letters in Words in a Story	
Number of Letters in Words	Frequency
1	
2	
3	
4	
5	
6	
7	
8	

Use the frequency table. How many words had:

1. 3 letters? _____
2. 2 letters? _____
3. 8 letters? _____
4. more than 3 letters? _____
5. less than 3 letters? _____

Name _____

Skills Practice

Collect and Organize Data

Organize the set of data in a frequency table.

1. Fernando took note of the types of pants worn by his classmates on a certain day. Below is his recording.

   Type of pants: jeans, corduroys, khaki, jeans, athletic pants, jeans, jeans, khaki, corduroys, corduroys, slacks, corduroys, cargo pants, cargo pants, jeans

Organize the set of data in a tally chart.

2. Types of pizza preferred by Coach Andretti's soccer team:

pepperoni	pepperoni
sausage	sausage
extra cheese	veggie
ham & pineapple	cheese
pepperoni	ham & pineapple

Reteach

Find Mode, Median, and Outliers

Median, Mode, and Outliers

You can analyze data using the median and mode. Use the table to help you find the outlier, median, and mode.

Outlier: an item of data that lies outside most of the data.

The outlier is 10

Median: the middle number when the data is arranged in order from least to greatest

1, 3, 5, 5, 10
   ↑

The median is 5.

Mode: the number that occurs most often

There are two 5s, so 5 is the mode.

Votes for Class President	
Student	**Number of Votes**
John	5
Carlos	10
Mike	3
Annie	1
Shavaughn	5

Order the data from *least* to *greatest*. Then find the median, mode, and outlier.

1. Data: 6, 4, 3, 3, 0, 5, 10

   List in order from least to greatest: ___, ___, ___, ___, ___, ___, ___

   Median: ___   Mode: ___   Outlier: ___

2. Data: 83, 96, 91, 83, 78

   List in order from least to greatest: ___, ___, ___, ___, ___

   Median: ___   Mode: ___   Outlier: ___

3. Data: 56, 88, 100, 34, 96, 56, 92

   List in order from least to greatest: ___, ___, ___, ___, ___, ___, ___

   Median: ___   Mode: ___   Outlier: ___

Name _____

Skills Practice

Find Mode, Median, and Outliers

Find the mode.

1. 9, 5, 4, 3, 4, 5, 7, 5 _____

2. 1, 2, 3, 5, 6, 4, 6, 7, 6 _____

3. 6, 4, 2, 1, 2, 4, 8, 4 _____

4. 3, 1, 5, 4, 3, 3, 1, 7, 6 _____

Find the median.

5. 4, 5, 1, 3, 3, 5, 1 _____

6. 8, 5, 4, 3, 6, 1, 8 _____

7. 2, 4, 1, 6, 7, 7, 3 _____

8. 1, 9, 3, 8, 7, 8, 1 _____

Identify the outlier in the data set.

9. 3, 5, 7, 9, 4, 20 _____

10. 9, 10, 3, 12, 11 _____

11. 16, 14, 13, 11, 10, 40 _____

12. 8, 9, 1, 11, 12, 10 _____

Find the mode and median of the data set. Identify any outliers.

13.

Pennies Found on the Sidewalk

Day	Pennies Found
1	8
2	8
3	12
4	1
5	7

Mode: _____

Median: _____

Outlier(s): _____

Name _____

Reteach

Problem-Solving Strategy: Make a Table

Which type of fish has the greatest number of varieties listed in the chart?

Varieties of Tetras, Goldfish, and Angelfish		
black neon tetra black moor goldfish gold angel lemon tetra	fantail goldfish white skirt tetra silver dollar tetra marble angel	lionhead goldfish diamond tetra silver angel

Step 1. Understand

Be sure you understand the problem.

Read carefully.

What do you know?
- There are different varieties of _____, _____, and
  _____.

What do you need to find?
- You need to know how many different varieties of _____,
  _____, and _____ are listed.

Step 2. Plan

- Make a table or list
- Work backward
- Find a pattern
- Guess and check
- Solve a simpler problem
- Write a number sentence
- Act it out
- Make a graph
- Use logical reasoning
- Draw a picture

Make a plan.

Choose a strategy.
A table can help you organize what you know.
Make a table to solve the problem.

Name _____

Reteach

Problem-Solving Strategy   (continued)

Step 3. Solve

Carry out your plan.

Make a table.

Tally the number of _____ for each fish. Write a number for each set of tallies. Compare the numbers.

Complete the table.

Type of Fish	Tally of Different Varieties	Total Tally
Tetras		
Goldfish	///	3
Angelfish		

There are _____ different kinds of tetras.

There are _____ different kinds of goldfish.

There are _____ different kinds of angelfish.

There are more varieties of _____ than either of the other two kinds of fish.

Step 4. Check

Is the answer reasonable?

Reread the problem.

Does your answer match the data given in the problem?

Practice

1. Jack lists the fish in his aquarium. He has a fantail goldfish, a lionhead goldfish, a gold angel angelfish, a lemon tetra, and a black neon tetra. Of which type of fish does Jack have the least?

_____

3-3

Skills Practice

Problem-Solving Strategy: Make a Table

Solve. Use the *make a table* strategy.

Favorite Kind of Pet			
Elliot—dog	Howard—dog	Jane—bird	Rebecca—bird
Marion—cat	Noriko—bird	Teri—cat	Melanie—cat
Tina—hamster	Yolanda—dog	Sarah—cat	Traci—dog
Paula—fish	Barry—cat	Bruce—dog	Noreen—fish
Sam—cat	Juan—dog	Mike—cat	Sylvia—cat

1. Which pet got the most votes? _____

2. Which pet got the fewest votes? _____

3. Marla earns $5 for mowing a lawn. If she mows 5 lawns a week for 4 weeks, how much money will she earn?

   _____

4. Devin's parents bought a computer for $1,800. If they pay $180 each month, how many months will it take them to pay for the computer?

   _____

5. Shondra invites 15 of her friends over for Yogurt. Nine of them want strawberry, five of them want vanilla. How many of Shondra's friends want a flavor other than strawberry or vanilla?

   _____

6. Aaron is having a birthday party and he wants to make gift bags for his friends. If he wants to invite 10 friends and wants to include 4 items in each bag. How many total items does he need?

   _____

7. If James earns $6 per hour, how many hours per week does he work if he makes $360 every 2 weeks?

   _____

8. Write a problem where make a table would help you to solve it.

   _____

3-4

Reteach

Line Plots

A line plot is another way to organize data. Line plots are a lot like tally charts. In line plots, you use Xs above a number line instead of tally marks next to a category. Line plots are used when you want to chart how often a certain number occurs in your data.

Students riding afterschool bus:

Day	Students
Monday	15
Tuesday	20
Wednesday	22
Thursday	20
Friday	21

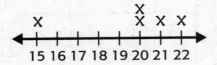

Mode: 20
Median: 20
Outlier: 15

Organize the set of data in a line plot.

1. Number of students in each classroom:

Teacher	Students
Mrs. Connolly	27
Mr. Martinez	32
Mrs. Jones	29
Mr. Washington	30
Mrs. Gematti	31
Mrs. Norris	29
Mr. Calderone	29
Mrs. Abalon	31
Mr. Selfani	36

Identify the mode, median, and outliers for the data set.

2. Number of students in classroom.

Mode: _____   Median: _____

Outlier: _____

Name _____

Skills Practice

Line Plots

Organize each set of data in a line plot.

1. Number of fans at the football game:

Game	Fans
1	49,000
2	47,000
3	52,000
4	50,000
5	51,000
6	52,000
7	52,000
8	48,000
9	36,000

2. Points scored by home team at each football game:

Game	Points
1	24
2	21
3	27
4	21
5	28
6	10
7	31
8	21
9	35

Identify the mode, median, and outliers for the data set.

3. Number of fans at the football game.

Mode: _____

Median: _____

Outlier: _____

4. Number of points scored by the home team at each football game.

Mode: _____

Median: _____

Outlier: _____

Name _____

Reteach

Bar Graphs

A **bar graph** is used to display data by using bars of different heights to represent values.

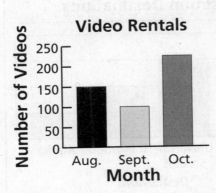

The bar graph shows the number of videos rented during three months of the year. Write two statements that describe the data.

The bar of October is the longest. So, you can write October had the most video rentals. The length of the bar for October is more than twice the length of the bar for September. So, you can write October has more than twice the number of video rentals than September.

For Exercise 1–2, use the graph shown.

The graph shows the number of items of furniture at a school.

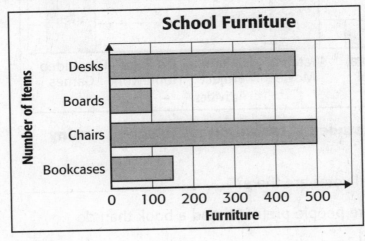

1. Which item does the school have the most of? _____

2. About how many more desks are there than bookcases? _____

Name _____

Skills Practice

Bar Graphs

For Exercises 1–5, use the graphs shown.

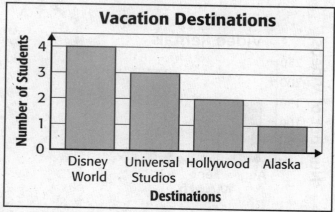

The graph shows students' vacation destinations.

1. Which vacation destination is the most popular?

_____

2. How many more students visited Universal Studios than Alaska? _____

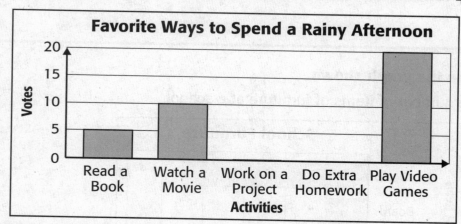

The graph shows students' favorite ways to spend a rainy afternoon.

3. How many total votes are there? _____

4. How many more people prefer to read a book than do

   extra homework? _____

5. What is the second most popular way to spend a rainy afternoon?

_____

3-6

Reteach

Bar and Double Bar Graphs

You can use single bar graphs or double bar graphs to show data. A single bar graph presents one set of data. A double bar graph presents two sets of related data.

When you read a double bar graph, you need to look at the key to see which kind of bar represents each set of data.

For Exercises 1–4, use the graphs shown.

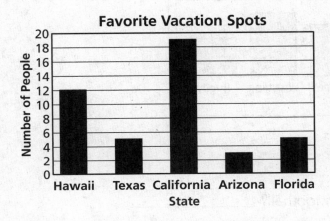

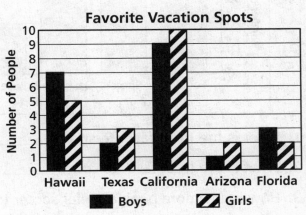

1. What is the favorite vacation spot? How many people chose it?

   _____

2. Did more people choose Arizona, Hawaii, or Texas as their favorite

   vacation spot? _____

3. How many more boys than girls chose Hawaii as their favorite

   vacation spot? _____

4. Which vacation spot shows the greatest difference between boys

   and girls? _____

Name _____

Skills Practice

Bar and Double Bar Graphs

For Exercises 1–3, use the bar graph that shows students favorite sports.

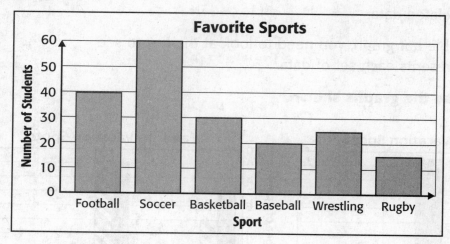

1. What is the most favorite sport? _____

2. What is the least favorite sport? _____

3. How many more people prefer soccer to football? _____

For Exercises 4–6, use the bar graph that shows votes received by the candidates for student body president.

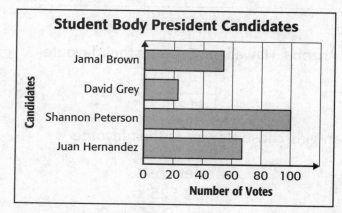

4. How many total students voted for student body president? _____

5. Which candidate is the winner of the election?

_____

6. How many more votes did David Grey need to win the election?

_____

Name _____

Reteach

Problem-Solving Investigation: Choose a Strategy

There are many ways to solve most math problems. You will decide which strategy works best for you when you read the problems. Here are problem-solving strategies and tips on when to use them.

Draw a picture: This strategy can help you look at the information in the problem a different way—useful when the problem is about distance or location.

Look for a pattern: This strategy can help you solve problems when the input changes.

Make a table: This strategy can help you solve problems that have a lot of information to organize.

Use this problem to learn more about choosing a strategy: Erin wants to buy bracelets for each of her friends. Each bracelet costs $3. If she has $25, how many bracelets can she buy?

Understand	You know that 1 bracelet costs $3. You know she has $25. You need to find out how many bracelets she can buy.
Plan	Choose a strategy. This problem has a lot of information that you must use to solve the problem. A table is a good way to organize information you have. Make a table to solve the problem.
Solve	*(table below)*

Bracelets	1	2	3	4	5	6	7	8	9
Cost of Bracelets	$3	$6	$9	$12	$15	$18	$21	$24	$27

You know how much 1 bracelet costs. You can fill in the chart to find out how many bracelets $25 can buy.
Erin can buy 8 bracelets.

Name _____

Reteach

Problem-Solving Investigation   (continued)

Check	Look back at the problem. Check to see if you are correct: 8 bracelets cost $24. 9 bracelets cost $27. $27 is more than $25. $25 is more than $24. Your answer is correct.

Use any strategy to solve. Tell what strategy you used.

1. Notebooks come with 50 pieces of paper. There are 32 students in class. If each student uses 5 pieces of paper, how many notebooks does the class need? _____

   Strategy: _____

2. Each batch of dough makes 6 rolls. If Sam wants to make 32 rolls, how many batches of dough will he need? _____

   Strategy: _____

3. Gabrielle is decorating cubes for her room. If she puts four cubes together against a wall and wants a different color on each visible side, how many different colors will she need? _____

   Strategy: _____

4. Laura is making a picnic. For every person coming to the picnic, she must have 2 sandwiches, 4 drinks, and 10 pretzels. If 4 people come to the picnic, how many food items will she need?

   _____

   Strategy: _____

3-7

Skills Practice

Problem-Solving Investigation: Choose a Strategy

Use any strategy to solve. Tell what strategy you used.

1. Admission to the skate park is $4 per child and $10 per adult. If Kristen's father brings Kristen and her friends to the skate park, how many friends can Kristen bring if they have $40 to spend?

   _____

   Strategy: _____

2. At the class party, each student brings two guests. If there are

   84 people at the party, how many are students? _____

   Strategy: _____

3. Connor is making squares out of toothpicks. Each square is formed from 4 toothpicks. If he has 13 toothpicks, how many squares can

   he build? _____

   Strategy: _____

4. Richard's class was collecting clothes to donate to the shelter. Richard brought 4 pieces. Jackie and Kelly each brought 6 pieces. Hunter brought 7 pieces, and Tim brought 5 pieces. How many pieces of clothing did Richard's class collect?

   _____

   Strategy: _____

5. Marissa is making a necklace. She uses these beads: blue, blue, purple, green, blue, blue... What color bead is next if this pattern

   continues? _____

   Strategy: _____

6. Copy and complete the number pattern.

   6, 9, 11, 14, 16, _____, _____, _____, _____

   Strategy: _____

3-8

Reteach

Determine Possible Outcomes

John is playing with a number cube and a penny. What are all the possible combinations of one roll of the cube and one flip of the penny?

Create a tree diagram or a grid to find all possible outcomes.

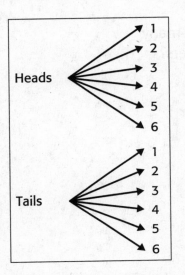

Penny Flip

Number Cube Roll	Heads	Tails
1	1, Heads	1, Tails
2	2, Heads	2, Tails
3	3, Heads	3, Tails
4	4, Heads	4, Tails
5	5, Heads	5, Tails
6	6, Heads	6, Tails

There are 12 possible outcomes.

Draw a tree diagram to show all the possible outcomes for the situation.

1. Choose a shirt and shorts.

Shirt	Shorts
Red	Blue
Orange	White
	Black

Skills Practice

Determine Possible Outcomes

Draw a tree diagram to show all the possible outcomes for the situation.

Spinner 1   Spinner 2

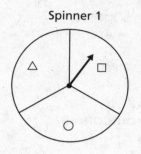   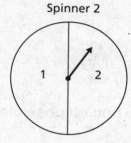

1. Jared and Dimitri are playing a game with 2 spinners. How many possible combinations are there if Dimitri spins both spinners?

_____ possible combinations

Draw a grid to show all the possible outcomes for the situation.

2. Anna is deciding what she could wear to the zoo tomorrow. She can choose a white shirt, a green shirt, or a blue shirt. She can choose blue pants or green pants. How many different outfits can

she make? _____ possible outfits

What are they?

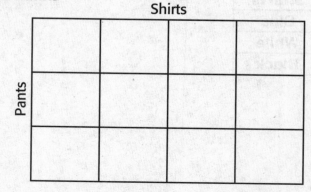

3-9

Reteach

Probability

The chance, or likelihood, that something will happen is called **probability**.

Look at the spinner at the right. You could spin 1, 2, 3, 4, 5, or 6. There are 6 possible outcomes.

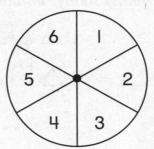

- The probability of spinning each number is **equally likely**.

- It is **impossible** to spin an 8.

- It is **certain** that you will spin a number greater than 0.

Look at the spinner at the right.

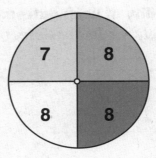

- The probability of spinning a 7 is **unlikely**.

- The probability of spinning an 8 is **likely**.

Look at the spinner at the right. Use the words *likely, equally likely, certain, unlikely,* or *impossible* to describe the probability.

1. The probability of spinning 12 is

_____.

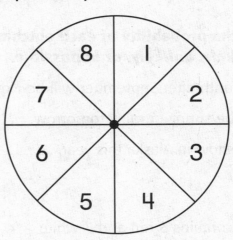

2. It is _____ that you will land on a number greater than 2.

3. It is _____ that you will land on a number less than 2.

4. It is _____ that you will land on a number less than 9.

5. It is _____

_____ that you will land on an odd or even number.

6. It is _____ to land on a number greater than 8.

Name _____

Skills Practice
Probability

**Describe the probability of picking a certain shape from the bag.
Use *certain, likely, equally likely, unlikely,* or *impossible*.**

1. ◯ _____

2. ⌂ _____

3. △ or □ _____

4. △, □ or ◯ _____

Describe the probability of each outcome. Use *certain, likely, equally likely, unlikely,* or *impossible*.

5. spinning 2 _____

6. spinning 3 _____

7. spinning 6 _____

8. spinning 1 _____

9. spinning 3 or 4 _____

10. spinning 1, 2, 3, or 4 _____

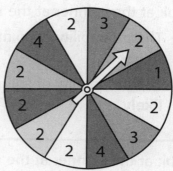

Describe the probability of each outcome. Use *certain, likely, equally likely, unlikely,* or *impossible*.

11. The month after September will be November. _____

12. It will be sunny or rainy tomorrow. _____

13. It will snow in Alaska this year. _____

Solve.

14. A bag contains 3 red and 7 white balls. Is it unlikely, more likely, or equally likely you will pick a red ball?

_____

15. A box contains 6 red pencils and 6 black pencils. Is it unlikely, less likely, or equally likely you will pick a red pencil?

_____

4-1 Reteach

Relate Multiplication and Division

The arrangement of blocks below is an example of an array. You can write a fact family to describe the array. A fact family is a set of four related multiplication and division sentences that use the same three numbers.

There are 3 rows, 5 columns, and a total of 15 blocks.
So, the fact family is:

$3 \times 5 = 15$ $5 \times 3 = 15$ $15 \div 3 = 5$ $15 \div 5 = 3$

Write a fact family for each array or set of numbers.

1. ☐☐☐☐☐☐ ☐☐☐☐☐☐ ☐☐☐☐☐☐

_____
_____
_____

2. ☐☐☐☐☐☐☐☐ ☐☐☐☐☐☐☐☐

_____
_____
_____

3. ☐☐☐ ☐☐☐ ☐☐☐ ☐☐☐

_____
_____
_____

4. ☐☐☐☐☐ ☐☐☐☐☐ ☐☐☐☐☐ ☐☐☐☐☐

_____
_____
_____

5. ☐☐☐☐☐☐☐ ☐☐☐☐☐☐☐

_____
_____
_____

6. ☐☐☐☐☐☐ ☐☐☐☐☐☐ ☐☐☐☐☐☐ ☐☐☐☐☐☐

_____
_____
_____

7. 6, 5, 30

_____
_____
_____

8. 3, 9, 27

_____
_____
_____

9. 7, 8, 56

_____
_____
_____

Name _____

Skills Practice

Relate Multiplication and Division

Write a fact family for each array.

1. ▢▢▢▢▢▢▢▢▢
   ▢▢▢▢▢▢▢▢▢

2. ▢▢▢
   ▢▢▢
   ▢▢▢
   ▢▢▢
   ▢▢▢

3. ▢▢▢▢
   ▢▢▢▢
   ▢▢▢▢

_____   _____   _____

_____   _____   _____

_____   _____   _____

Divide. Use a related multiplication fact.

4. $6 \div 2 =$ ___

5. $7\overline{)42} =$ ___

6. $8\overline{)56}$ ___

7. $18 \div 2 =$ ___

8. $3\overline{)21}$ ___

9. $9\overline{)45}$ ___

10. $15 \div 5 =$ ___

11. $7\overline{)21}$ ___

12. $9\overline{)81}$ ___

13. $8 \div 4 =$ ___

14. $2\overline{)16}$ ___

15. $9\overline{)36}$ ___

16. $27 \div 3 =$ ___

17. $3\overline{)18}$ ___

18. $8\overline{)64}$ ___

19. $14 \div 2 =$ ___

20. $5\overline{)25}$ ___

21. $9\overline{)72}$ ___

22. $28 \div 7 =$ ___

23. $5\overline{)45}$ ___

24. $6\overline{)54}$ ___

25. $36 \div 6 =$ ___

26. $7\overline{)56}$ ___

27. $4\overline{)24}$ ___

Solve.

28. It takes 4 horses to pull a coach. How many coaches can

    20 horses pull? _____

29. Groups of 6 visitors can take tours of an old western town.

    How many groups can 24 people make? _____

Reteach

Algebra: Multiplication Properties and Division Rules

Commutative Property of Multiplication	**Associative Property of Multiplication**
The order of the factors does not change the answer.	The way factors are grouped does not change the answer.

The order of the factors does not change the answer.

$4 \times 2 = 8$ $2 \times 4 = 8$

The way factors are grouped does not change the answer.

$(4 \times 2) \times 3 = 24$

$4 \times (2 \times 3) = 24$

Identity Property of Multiplication	**Zero Property of Multiplication**

The product of 1 and any number is that number.

$3 \times 1 = 3$

$1 \times 6 = 6$

The product of any number and zero is zero.

Think: 4 rows of 0 counters.

$4 \times 0 = 0$

Think: 0 rows of 7 counters.

$0 \times 7 = 0$

Identify the property shown by each number sentence.

1. $3 \times 9 = 9 \times 3$

_____

_____

2. $(5 \times 7) \times 2 = 5 \times (7 \times 2)$

_____

_____

3. $4 \times 0 = 0$

_____

_____

4. $2 \times 8 = 8 \times 2$

_____

_____

5. $1 \times 4 = 4$

_____

_____

6. $0 \times 5 = 0$

_____

_____

Name _____

Skills Practice

Algebra: Multiplication Properties and Division Rules

Copy and complete each number sentence. Identify the property used.

1. $9 \times 8 =$ ____ $\times 9$

   _____

2. $9 \times$ ____ $= 0$

   _____

3. $6 \times (9 \times 5) = ($ ____ $\times 9) \times 5$

   _____

4. $8 \times 1 =$ ____

   _____

5. $3 \times 4 =$ ____ $\times 3$

   _____

6. $0 \times 3 =$ ____

   _____

Identify the property shown by each number sentence.

7. $5 \times (2 \times 4) = (5 \times 2) \times 4$

   _____

8. $8 \div 8 = 1$ _____

9. $5 \times 4 = 4 \times 5$

   _____

10. $1 \times 3 = 3$ _____

11. $4 \times 0 = 0$ _____

Solve.

12. Joe plants pine seedlings in 7 rows. He puts 6 seedlings in each row. How many seedlings does Joe plant?

    _____

13. Tanya has 54 pencils altogether. She has 6 packages. How many pencils are in each package?

    _____

4-3

Reteach

Multiply and Divide Facts Through 5

You can double a fact you know to multiply by 5.

Double a fact you already know to multiply by 5.

$4 \times 5 = (2 \times 5) + (2 \times 5)$

$$\downarrow \qquad \downarrow$$

10 + 10 = 20

•••••   •••••   •••••
••••• + ••••• = •••••
                    •••••
                    •••••

Find 40 ÷ 5.   Think: How many groups of 5 are in 40?

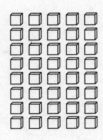

$5 \times ? = 40 \rightarrow 5 \times 8 = 40$
There are 8 groups of 5 in 40.   So, $40 \div 5 = 8$.

Multiply or divide.

1. $5 \times 8 =$ _____

2. $4 \times 7 =$ _____

3. $7 \times 5 =$ _____

4. $8 \times 4 =$ _____

5. $12 \div 2 =$ _____

6. $21 \div 3 =$ _____

7. $20 \div 5 =$ _____

8. $14 \div 2 =$ _____

9. $24 \div 4 =$ _____

10. $16 \div 2 =$ _____

11. $2 \times 5 =$ _____

12. $5 \times 5 =$ _____

13. $3 \times 8 =$ _____

14. $5 \times 6 =$ _____

15. $4 \times 9 =$ _____

16. $4\overline{)32} =$ _____

17. $5\overline{)50} =$ _____

18. $3\overline{)36} =$ _____

4-3

Skills Practice

Multiply and Divide Facts Through 5

Multiply or divide.

1. 2×8 ___

2. 10×5 ___

3. $5 \div 1$ ___

4. 5×4 ___

5. 3×3 ___

6. $12 \div 3$ ___

7. 4×1 ___

8. 5×2 ___

9. $6 \div 2$ ___

10. 0×5 ___

11. 4×4 ___

12. $15 \div 3$ ___

ALGEBRA Complete each number sentence.

13. ☐ $\times 4 = 20$

14. ☐ $\div 5 = 10$

15. $2 \times 5 =$ ☐

16. $44 \div$ ☐ $= 4$

ALGEBRA Solve.

17.

There are 4 boxes of markers in a class. There are 20 students in the class. How many students share each box of markers?

_____

18. Sam is having a party with 18 of his friends. If 3 people can swing on the swing set at one time, how many groups will have to take turns?

_____

19. Brian has 4 packs of seeds to plant. If he uses one pack in a row, how many rows will he fill? _____

20. A clown has two bunches of flowers. Each bunch has 7 flowers in it. How many total flowers does the clown have? _____

21. Rosita has 40 stickers. If each pack of stickers has 8, how many packs of stickers does she have? _____

4-4

Reteach

Problem-Solving Strategy: Choose an Operation

Choose an Operation

Nadia collects souvenir flags. She puts the flags in her bookcase. The flags take up three rows. There are 7 flags in each row. How many flags does Nadia have?

Step 1. Understand
Be sure you understand the problem.
What do you know?
• Nadia has _____ rows of flags.
• There are _____ flags in each row.
What do you need to find?
• Total number of flags.

Step 2. Plan
Choose an operation.
To find the total of 3 equal groups of flags, you can use repeated addition or multiplication. Use multiplication because it is faster.

Step 3. Solve
Follow your plan.
Find how many flags Nadia has.
Nadia puts the flags in 3 rows. There are 7 flags in each row.
$3 \times 7 = 21$
Nadia has 21 flags.

Step 4. Check
Look back at the problem.
Use repeated addition.
$7 + 7 + 7 = 21$

Tell which operation you would use to solve each problem. Then solve.

I. Janell has 472 baseball cards. Lou has 397 baseball cards. How many more baseball cards does Janell have than Lou?

4-4

Reteach

Problem-Solving Strategy (continued)

2. Kevin buys 7 packs of football cards. There are 4 football cards in each pack. How many football cards does Kevin buy?

   _____

3. Brian displays his trophies in his bedroom. He puts his trophies in 3 rows. There are 6 trophies in each row. How many trophies does Brian have?

   _____

4. Barbara puts photos of France in a photo album. The photo album can hold 94 photos. Barbara has 78 photos. How many more photos can she put in the album?

   _____

5. Amad has 4 rows of sock pairs in his drawer. Each row has 8 pairs. How many pairs does Kevin have in all?

   _____

6. Li Cheng puts his comic books into 8 airtight bins. If each bin can hold 8 comic books, how many comic books does Li Cheng have?

   _____

7. Teresa has 900 stickers. Her sister Maria has 727. How many more stickers does Teresa have than her sister?

   _____

8. Ms. Hernandez has 40 roses to share equally with each girl in her class. If each girl gets 5 roses, how many girls are in the class?

   _____

9. If you have 30 points, but need 179 in order to win a prize, how many more points do you need?

   _____

10. Sheryl has 4 apples. If she gives none of them away, how many does she have left?

    _____

4-4

Skills Practice

Problem-Solving Strategy: Choose an Operation

**Tell which operation you would use to solve each problem.
Then solve.**

1. Georgia puts coins in an album. There are 8 pages in the album. Each page has slots for 8 coins. How many coins can Georgia put in the album? _____

2. Dina has 37 international dolls. Maxine has 26 international dolls. Who has more dolls? How many more does she have?

_____

3. Ben buys 9 packs of dinosaur stickers. There are 6 stickers in each pack. How many stickers does Ben buy? _____

_____

4. Melanie has a collection of 242 stamps. At a stamp convention, she buys 19 more stamps. How many stamps does Melanie have now? _____

5. James collects model cars. He has 48 model cars. On his birthday, James gets 7 more cars. How many model cars does James have in all?

_____

6. Lucy fills a basket with apples. She put 16 apples in the basket. A total of 28 apples will fit. How many more apples can Lucy put in the basket?

_____

4–5

Reteach

Multiply and Divide Facts Through 10

Multiply

Find 4×5.
Think: Skip count by 5s four times.

You can skip count with nickels to multiply by 5.

  5   10   15   20

$$4 \times 5 = 20$$

Divide

Find $30 \div 6$.
Think: How many groups of 6 are in 30?

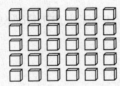

$$6 \times ? = 30 \rightarrow 5 \times 6 = 30$$
There are 5 groups of 6 in 30. So, $30 \div 6 = 5$.

Multiply or divide.

1. $7 \times 5 =$ _____

2. $21 \div 3 =$ _____

3. $10\overline{)30}$ _____

4. $8 \times 6 =$ _____

5. $20 \div 5 =$ _____

6. $11\overline{)33}$ _____

7. $9 \times 8 =$ _____

8. $12 \div 2 =$ _____

9. $12\overline{)36}$ _____

10. $\begin{array}{r} 5 \\ \times\, 8 \\ \hline \end{array}$

11. $\begin{array}{r} 10 \\ \times\, 9 \\ \hline \end{array}$

12. $\begin{array}{r} 6 \\ \times\, 6 \\ \hline \end{array}$

Name _____

Skills Practice

Multiply and Divide Facts Through 10

1. 6 × 8 _____

2. 8 ÷ 2 _____

3. 8)‾80‾ _____

4. 7 × 4 _____

5. 15 ÷ 3 _____

6. 7)‾56‾ _____

7. 4 × 10 _____

8. 80 ÷ 8 _____

9. 6)‾42‾ _____

10. 0 × 7 _____

11. 21 ÷ 3 _____

12. 5)‾45‾ _____

13.   9
     × 6

14.   8
     × 3

15.   6
     × 2

16.   3
     × 9

ALGEBRA Solve.

17. Kia has 48 apples to split evenly into 4 gift baskets. How many apples will fit into each basket?

_____

18. Jan is making bracelets for her friends. She is using 10 beads for each bracelet. How many beads will she use if she makes 7 bracelets?

_____

19. Amy scored 8 points in her basketball game. If she scored the same number of points in the next 3 games, how many points did she score altogether?

_____

20. Laura bought 2 grapefruits for each of her 3 friends. If each grapefruit has 10 pieces, how many pieces will there be in all?

_____

4-6

Reteach

Multiply with 11 and 12

You can use a related multiplication fact to find the quotient to a division problem.

Elliot and 6 of his friends go to Happy Land Park. The total for all of their tickets was $77. How much did each person pay for his ticket?

Use a related multiplication fact to help you find $77 ÷ 7.

```
THINK 7 × $ ___ = $77
      7 × $11 = $77
```

$77 ÷ 7 = $11   So, the cost of each ticket was $11.

You can also use either repeated addition or arrays to multiply.

At the store, how many dozen muffins are in a tray of 72?
Find how many dozens of muffins there are in 72 by finding

_____ × 12 = 72.

Skip count by 12s or add 12 six times.

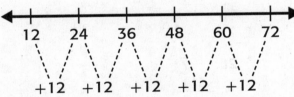

12 + 12 + 12 + 12 + 12 + 12 = 72   So, 6 × 12 = 72

Multiply or divide.

1. 12 × 7 _____

2. 11 × 11 _____

3. 110 ÷ 11 _____

4. 88 ÷ 11 _____

5. 3 × 12 _____

6. 10 × 6 _____

7. Art students were making frames out of craft sticks. Each frame uses 11 sticks. If there are 44 total sticks, how many frames can they make?

_____

4-6

Skills Practice

Multiply with 11 and 12

1. 11×8 _____

2. $12 \div 2$ _____

3. 7×12 _____

4. $33 \div 3$ _____

5. 4×11 _____

6. $88 \div 8$ _____

7. 10×6 _____

8. $72 \div 12$ _____

9. $5\overline{)55}$ _____

10. $12\overline{)96}$ _____

11. $11\overline{)44}$ _____

12. $5\overline{)60}$ _____

13. $\begin{array}{r} 10 \\ \times 5 \\ \hline \end{array}$

14. $\begin{array}{r} 11 \\ \times 3 \\ \hline \end{array}$

15. $\begin{array}{r} 10 \\ \times 2 \\ \hline \end{array}$

16. $\begin{array}{r} 11 \\ \times 9 \\ \hline \end{array}$

17. $\begin{array}{r} 12 \\ \times 5 \\ \hline \end{array}$

18. $\begin{array}{r} 3 \\ \times 12 \\ \hline \end{array}$

19. $\begin{array}{r} 12 \\ \times 8 \\ \hline \end{array}$

20. $\begin{array}{r} 7 \\ \times 11 \\ \hline \end{array}$

ALGEBRA Solve.

21. Kim has 12 people over for a party. Each table can seat 4 people. How many tables will she need? _____

22. Jennifer is making key chains for her family. She is using 11 beads for each key chain. How many beads will she use if she makes 6 key chains? _____

Name _____

Reteach

Problem-Solving Investigation: Choose a Strategy

To practice making sharper turns, Camille sets up an obstacle course. She places cones 3 feet apart over a distance of 20 yards. She places the first cone 3 feet from the starting line. How many cones does Camille use?

Step 1 Understand

Be sure you understand the problem.
Read carefully.

What do you know?
• The cones are spread over a distance of _____ yards.

• Camille begins 3 feet from the starting line and places cones _____ feet apart.

What do you need to find?
• You need to find the number of feet in _____ yards.

• You need to find how many _____.

Step 2 Plan

• Logical reasoning
• Make a graph
• Make a table or list
• Guess and check
• Work backward

• Draw a picture or diagram
• Act it out
• Find a pattern
• Write an equation
• Solve a simpler problem

Make a plan.

Choose a strategy.
To find the answer, you can draw a diagram.
Find the number of feet in 20 yards.
Show a distance that is that many feet long.
Count by 3s to see how many cones Camille uses if they are placed 3 feet apart.
To find the answer, you can also write an equation.
All the cones are the same distance apart.
Use division to find how many cones Camille uses.

Name _____

Reteach

Problem-Solving Investigation (continued)

Step 3 Solve

Carry out your plan.

How many feet are in 20 yards?

1 yard = 3 feet

$20 \times 3 = 60$

Draw a diagram. Show a 60-foot distance. Count by 3s, adding tick marks as shown.

$\vdash\!\!+\!\!\dashv$

0 6 12 18 24 30 36 42 48 54 60 66 72 78 84 90 96 102 108 114 120 126 132 138 144 150

Count the tick marks from 3 to 60. Camille uses _____ cones.

You could also write an equation.

The distance is _____ feet. There will be 1 cone every _____ feet.

Write a division equation. _____ ÷ _____ = _____

Camille uses _____ cones.

Step 4 Check

Is the solution reasonable?

Reread the problem.

Does your answer make sense?   Yes   No
Which method do you prefer? Explain.

_____

_____

Solve.

1. The parks department builds 5 rows of stands next to a baseball field. Each row is 20 feet long. How many 10-foot-long boards did they need to build the stands? _____

2. Ed has 4 packs of sports stickers. There are 24 stickers in each pack. He divides the stickers among 3 friends. How many stickers does each friend get? _____

Name _____

Skills Practice

Problem-Solving Investigation: Choose a Strategy

Use the make a table strategy or choose an operation to solve each problem.

1. The Sports Committee buys 30 yards of material. The material is cut into banners that are 5 feet long. How many banners are

   made? _____

2. The Sand Trap Golf Shop has 132 golf balls in stock. The golf balls are packed in tubes of 6. How many tubes of golf balls does the

   store have? _____

3. Liam is building a fence around his entire backyard. The backyard is 24 feet wide and 60 feet long. If Liam uses sections of fencing that are

   12 feet long, how many sections does he use? _____

4. There are 115 students going to the basketball tournament. Each bus

   can carry 26 students. How many buses are needed? _____

5. Tina makes a display of 36 autographed baseballs. She puts 12 baseballs in a large display case. Tina also has 4 smaller display cases. How can she arrange the baseballs in the smaller cases so that each smaller case has an equal number of baseballs?

   _____

   _____

6. Francine uses a pattern to make a window display for a sneaker store. The first row has 2 sneakers, the second row has 6 sneakers, the third row has 10, and the fourth row has 14. How many

   sneakers are in the fifth row? _____

7. The Stadium Store sells 450 team photos and 369 individual

   photos. How many photos does it sell in all? _____

8. Write a problem that you could solve by drawing a diagram or by writing a division sentence. Share it with others.

   _____

Name _____

Reteach

Algebra: Multiply Three Numbers

You can use the Associative Property of Multiplication to multiply more than two numbers.

CAT FOOD CAT FOOD

If you have 3 cats and they each eat 2 cans of food per day, how many cans do they eat in 1 week?

You need to find $3 \times 2 \times 7$.

You will multiply two of the facts together at a time.

$(3 \times 2) \times 7$ or $3 \times (2 \times 7)$

$6 \quad \times 7$ $3 \times \quad 14$

42 42

Either way they will eat 42 cans of food in 1 week.

Multiply.

1. $4 \times 6 \times 2$ _____

2. $8 \times 1 \times 5$ _____

3. $12 \times 6 \times 3$ _____

4. $7 \times 3 \times 1$ _____

5. $9 \times 5 \times 3$ _____

6. $11 \times 4 \times 2$ _____

ALGEBRA Copy and complete each number sentence.

7. $3 \times \boxed{} \times 3 = 63$

8. $4 \times 8 \times 4 = \boxed{}$

9. $8 \times 2 \times \boxed{} = 16$

10. $7 \times \boxed{} \times 6 = 210$

Name _____

Skills Practice

Algebra: Multiply Three Numbers

Multiply.

1. $3 \times 1 \times 6 =$ _____

2. $8 \times 4 \times 2 =$ _____

3. $4 \times 2 \times 7 =$ _____

4. $7 \times 9 \times 3 =$ _____

5. $9 \times 6 \times 4 =$ _____

6. $11 \times 12 \times 1 =$ _____

ALGEBRA Copy and complete each number sentence.

7. $2 \times \square \times 4 = 64$ _____

8. $7 \times 3 \times \square = 210$ _____

9. $5 \times 4 \times 6 = \square$ _____

10. $10 \times 11 \times \square = 660$ _____

11. If you own 2 birds and they each eat 1 cup of seeds per week, how many cups of seed do they eat in 6 weeks?

_____

12.

You buy 2 notebooks, 4 pencils, and 5 erasers. For $1 each, how much

would you pay for all the items? _____

4-9

Reteach

Factors and Multiples

Laura is arranging her photos. She has 14 photos to arrange in a frame. How many ways can she arrange them?

You need to find all the factors of 14 to find out how many ways Laura can arrange her pictures.

Factors are numbers that divide into a whole number evenly. You will find number pairs that make a product of 14.

$1 \times 14 = 14$ 					$2 \times 7 = 14$

So, the factors of 14 are 1, 2, 7, and 14. The different arrays show two ways that the pictures can be arranged.

A **multiple** is the product of that number and a whole number. For example, 10 is a multiple of 2 because $5 \times 2 = 10$.

Find the first 7 multiples of 3.

On a multiplication table, look across the row for 3 or down the column for 3. All of the numbers listed in the row or column are multiples of 3.

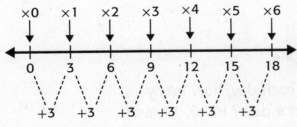

So, the first 7 multiples of 3 are 0, 3, 6, 9, 12, 15 and 18.

Find all of the factors of each number.

1. 5 _____   2. 8 _____   3. 13 _____

Identify the first five non-zero multiples for each number.

4. 2 ___, ___, ___, ___, _____   Think: $2 \times 1, 2 \times 2, 2 \times 3, 2 \times 4, 2 \times 5$

5. 4 ___, ___, _____, _____, _____   Think: $4 \times 1, 4 \times 2, 4 \times 3, 4 \times 4, 4 \times 5$

6. 6 ___, _____, _____, _____, _____   Think: $6 \times 1, 6 \times 2, 6 \times 3, 6 \times 4, 6 \times 5$

Name _____

Skills Practice

Factors and Multiples

Find all of the factors of each number.

1. 3 _____

2. 5 _____

3. 12 _____

4. 18 _____

5. 22 _____

6. 34 _____

Identify the first five multiples for each number.

7. 4 ____, ____, ____, ____, ____

8. 5 ____, ____, ____, ____, ____

9. 8 ____, ____, ____, ____, ____

10. 11 ____, ____, ____, ____, ____

11. 7 ____, ____, ____, ____, ____

12. 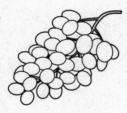 If you eat 10 grapes each day, how many grapes will you eat in 9 days? In 10, 11, and 12 days?____, ____, ____, ____

13. Each music class sings 8 songs a day for 5 days a week. How many songs does each class sing in 5 weeks? 8 weeks? 10 weeks?

   _____, _____, _____

5-1

Reteach

Addition and Subtraction Expressions

A variable is used in an expression to represent an unknown number. In the expression $5 + x$, the unknown number is represented by the variable x.

You can find the value of an expression by substituting different numbers for the variable.

Find the value of $5 + x$ if $x = 2$. $5 + x$ $5 + 2 = 7$ So, the value of $5 + x$ if $x = 2$ is 7.	Find the value of $5 + x$ if $x = 5$. $5 + x$ $5 + 5 = 10$ So, the value of $5 + x$ if $x = 5$ is 10.
Find the value of $m - 3$ when $m = 7$. $m - 3$ $7 - 3 = 4$ So, the value of $m - 3$ when $m = 7$ is 4.	Find the value of $m - 3$ when $m = 10$. $m - 3$ $10 - 3 = 7$ So, the value of $m - 3$ when $m = 10$ is 7.

Find the value of each expression.

1. $m + 1$ when $m = 1$ _____

2. $z + 25$ if $z = 10$ _____

3. $5 + s$ if $s = 3$ _____

4. $30 + p$ when $p = 20$ _____

5. $7 - y$ when $y = 2$ _____

6. $31 - b$ if $b = 15$ _____

7. $25 \div (b + 3)$ when $b = 2$ _____

8. $k + 58$ when $k = 29$ _____

9. $c + 4$ if $c = 5$ _____

10. $e + 62$ if $e = 11$ _____

11. $f - 1$ when $f = 6$ _____

12. $r - 39$ when $r = 80$ _____

13. $a - 7$ if $a = 8$ _____

14. $p - 126$ when $p = 143$ _____

15. $8 + d$ when $d = 0$ _____

16. $252 + n$ if $n = 47$ _____

Name _____

Skills Practice

Addition and Subtraction Expressions

Find the value of each expression.

1. $9 - y$ if $y = 2$ _____

2. $71 - b$ when $b = 29$ _____

3. $m + 3$ if $m = 2$ _____

4. $k + 33$ when $k = 48$ _____

5. $3 + x$ when $x = 10$ _____

6. $p - 109$ if $p = 275$ _____

7. $12 - w$ when $w = 4$ _____

8. $288 + n$ when $n = 106$ _____

9. $z + 37$ if $z = 29$ _____

10. $121 + g$ if $g = 129$ _____

11. $54 + p$ when $p = 3$ _____

12. $500 - t$ if $t = 266$ _____

Write an expression for each situation.

13. 7 more than x _____

14. 12 and y more _____

15. 5 and p more _____

16. 25 and b more _____

17. 2 and m more _____

18. 155 more than q _____

19. 3 more than g _____

20. 341 and f more _____

Write an expression for the pattern.

21. $10 + 1$, $10 + 2$, $10 + 3$, ... _____

22. $45 - 5$, $45 - 6$, $45 - 7$, ... _____

23. $62 + 3$, $62 + 4$, $62 + 5$, ... _____

Solve.

24. George earns $30 plus tips each day. Write an expression to show his total daily pay. If George received $8 in tips yesterday, how much did he earn in all?

_____

25. Tanesha has 24 marbles. She gives away x number of marbles. Write an expression for the number of marbles she has left.

_____

Name _____

Reteach

Solve Equations Mentally

You can use compensation to add and subtract mentally when one number is close to a ten or a hundred. Add or subtract the same number from both numbers.

$$95 \rightarrow 97$$
$$-28 \rightarrow -30$$
$$\overline{ \ \ 67}$$

• Add 2 to 28 to make 30: $28 + 2 = 30$.
• Add 2 to the other number: $95 + 2 = 97$.

$$103 \rightarrow 100$$
$$-45 \rightarrow -42$$
$$\overline{ \ \ 58}$$

• Subtract 3 from 103 to make 100: $103 - 3 = 100$.
• Subtract 3 from 45: $45 - 3 = 42$.

$$197 \rightarrow 200$$
$$+254 \rightarrow +251$$
$$\overline{ \ \ 451}$$

• Add 3 to make 200: $197 + 3 = 200$.
• Subtract 3 from the other number: $254 - 3 = 251$.

Solve each equation mentally.

1. $26 - n = 19$ _____

2. $62 + 39 =$ _____

3. $84 - n = 52$ _____

4. $54 + 17 =$ _____

5. $79 - n = 48$ _____

6. $202 + 248 =$ _____

7. $\$58 - \$17 =$ _____

8. $\$316 + \$455 =$ _____

9. $94 - 38 =$ _____

10. $\$625 + \$330 =$ _____

11. $86 - 24 =$ _____

12. $437 + 128 =$ _____

13. $196 - 49 =$ _____

14. $499 + 252 =$ _____

15. $\$253 - \$42 =$ _____

16. $697 + 140 =$ _____

17. $395 - 91 =$ _____

18. $\$29 + \$56 =$ _____

19. $888 - 277 =$ _____

20. $\$62 + \$78 =$ _____

83

Name _____

Skills Practice

Solve Equations Mentally

Solve each equation mentally.

1. 32 + 45 = _____

2. 495 − 238 = _____

3. 21 + 64 = _____

4. 730 − 214 = _____

5. 35 + 13 = _____

6. 891 − 108 = _____

7. $39 + $24 = _____

8. $256 − $222 = _____

9. 48 + 31 = _____

10. 4,524 − 3,173 = _____

11. 298 + 311 = _____

12. 8,999 − 1,333 = _____

13. 595 + 409 = _____

14. 2,295 − 2,124 = _____

15. 255 + 344 = _____

16. 1,511 − 1,487 = _____

Write the value of each missing number.

17. $36 + a = 86$ _____

18. $b + 61 = 81$ _____

19. $498 + c = $698 _____

20. $d + 298 = 598$ _____

21. $e + 657 = 957$ _____

22. $63 + h = $243 _____

23. $725 + k = $1,125 _____

Solve.

24. The pet show committee spends $316 on dog treats and $299 on cat treats. How much does the committee spend on treats?

_____

5-3

Reteach

Problem-Solving Skill: Extra and Missing Information

A problem is **missing information** when you cannot solve it unless you have more information. A problem has **extra information** when it gives more information than needed to solve it.

Missing Information

Problem Jack started his homework at 4:15 P.M. and finished at 5:30 P.M. Jenny started her homework at 4:00 P.M. Who spent more time doing their homework, Jack or Jenny?

You cannot solve the problem unless you know when Jenny finished her homework.

Extra Information

Problem Sue started raking leaves at 2:00 P.M. and finished at 3:10 P.M. She then started practicing her violin and finished at 3:35 P.M. How long did Sue take to rake the leaves?

To solve the problem, you do not need to know how long it took Sue to practice.

Choose the correct answer.

Flight 81 leaves Salt Lake City at 2:55 P.M. and arrives in Phoenix at 4:30 P.M. Flight 62 from Salt Lake City, which is sold out, arrives in Phoenix at 3:45 P.M. Which flight is faster?

1. Which of the following statements is false?

   A. Flight 81 takes less than 2 hours.

   B. Flight 62 arrives in Phoenix after Flight 81 does.

   C. Flight 62 is sold out.

   D. Flight 81 arrives in Phoenix before 5:00 P.M.

   1. _____

2. What information is missing?

   F. the time that Flight 81 leaves Salt Lake City

   G. the time that Flight 81 arrives in Phoenix

   H. the time that Flight 62 leaves Salt Lake City

   J. the time that Flight 62 arrives in Salt Lake City

   2. _____

Name _____

Reteach (continued)

Problem-Solving Skill: Extra and Missing Information

An express train leaves Grand Terminal at 5:05 P.M. The train arrives at the first stop at 5:21 P.M., the second stop at 5:46 P.M., and the last stop at 6:04 P.M. How long is the train ride?

3. What information is not needed?

   A. the time the train leaves Grand Terminal

   B. the time the train arrives at the second stop

   C. the time the train arrives at the last stop

   D. none of the above

3. _____

4. How long is the train ride?

   F. 16 minutes

   G. 41 minutes

   H. 59 minutes

   J. 61 minutes

4. _____

Circle the question in each problem. Underline the needed facts. Identify the missing or extra information. Then solve if possible.

5. Sally eats three turkey sandwiches and two ham sandwiches a week. She eats at 12:30 every day. How many turkey sandwiches does she eat in two weeks?

   _____

   _____

   _____

6. Jill is 9 years old and she downloads 10 songs a month. How much does she spend after 3 months?

   _____

   _____

7. There are a total of 30 students. Twelve of them want chocolate ice cream. How many of them prefer strawberry?

   _____

   _____

5-3

Skills Practice

Problem-Solving Skill: Extra and Missing Information

Identify any extra or missing information. Then solve if possible.

1. A round-trip first-class ticket from St. Louis to San Diego costs $1,600. A round-trip coach ticket costs $359. The Howards buy 3 tickets. How much do they spend?

   _____

   _____

2. A train leaves Rocky Mount, NC, at 1:16 P.M. The train arrives in Petersburg, VA, at 2:45 P.M. and in Richmond, VA, at 3:22 P.M. How long is the trip from Rocky Mount to Richmond?

   _____

   _____

3. A bus leaves the terminal at 6:10 P.M. It makes its first stop at 6:30 P.M. and its second stop at 6:55 P.M. When will the bus arrive at its third stop?

   _____

   _____

4. Samantha takes a train to New York City. She catches the train at 7:25 A.M. The train stops in Newark at 7:41 A.M. The train arrives in New York at 7:59 A.M. How much time does Samantha's ride take?

   _____

   _____

Solve. Use any strategy.

5. Denzel has 3 rows of shelves in his bedroom. Books, games, or CDs occupy each shelf. The middle shelf holds CDs. If the top shelf

   does not hold books, which shelf holds games? _____

   Strategy: _____

6. Arlene spent $30 for a jacket. She now has $5 left. How much

   money did Arlene have before she bought the jacket? _____

   Strategy: _____

5-4

Reteach

Identify, Describe, and Extend Patterns

Jasmine bought 4 tickets for $12 and 5 tickets for $15. If the price of the tickets stays the same, how much will 7 tickets cost?

A **pattern** is a series of numbers or figures that follow a rule. In the situation above there is a pattern of how much each ticket costs.

Find the cost of one ticket by dividing the cost by the number of tickets. Since 4 tickets cost $12, we can see that one ticket will cost $3.
$12 \div 4 = 3$

We can check this by using the rest of the information.
Since 5 tickets cost $15, then one ticket will cost $3. $15 \div 5 = 3$
Use a pattern to find how much 7 tickets will cost.

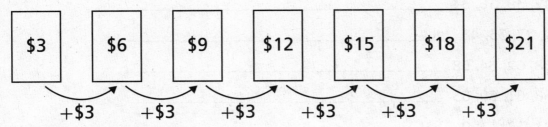

So, seven tickets will lost $21.

Find the rule for each pattern.

1. 15, 16, 13, 14, 11, 12 _____

2. 4, 9, 14, 19, 24, 29 _____

3. 24, 20, 16, 12, 8, 4 _____

4. 14, 20, 26, 32, 38, 44 _____

Find the next number in each pattern.

5. 6, 12, 18, 24, 30, ☐

6. 13, 15, 12, 14, 11, ☐

7. 54, 51, 48, 45, 42, ☐

8. 27, 23, 19, 15, 11, ☐

Name _____

Skills Practice

Identify, Describe, and Extend Patterns

Find the rule for each pattern.

1. 34, 41, 48, 55, 62, 69 _____

2. 13, 17, 21, 25, 29, 33 _____

3. 87, 76, 65, 54, 43, 32 _____

4. 23, 28, 25, 30, 27, 32 _____

5. 4, 10, 16, 22, 28, 34 _____

6. 5, 9, 8, 12, 11, 15 _____

7. 9, 6, 10, 7, 11, 8 _____

8. 48, 45, 42, 39, 36, 33 _____

9. 3, 11, 19, 27, 35, 43 _____

10. 72, 66, 68, 62, 64, 58 _____

11. 56, 59, 58, 61, 60, 63 _____

12. 29, 25, 21, 17, 13, 9 _____

Find the next number in each pattern.

13. 4, 8, 12, 16, 20, ☐

14. 64, 64, 62, 62, 60, ☐

15. 25, 29, 25, 29, 25, ☐

16. 25, 20, 15, 10, 5, ☐

17. 15, 21, 27, 33, 39, ☐

18. 40, 44, 43, 47, 46, ☐

19. 33, 44, 55, 66, 77, ☐

20. 50, 48, 46, 44, 42, ☐

21. 63, 54, 45, 36, 27, ☐

22. 13, 18, 23, 28, 33, ☐

23. 9, 13, 17, 21, 25, ☐

24. 69, 59, 49, 39, 29, ☐

25. Anwar reads every day. Based on the chart below, how many pages does Anwar read everyday?

Reading Log					
Day	1	2	3	4	5
Pages	25	50	75	100	125

_____

Name _____

Reteach

Function Tables: Find a Rule (+, −)

Sometimes math exercises have a pattern to the answers. Once you find the pattern, you can make a rule that will solve the problem for any input.

Use this problem to learn more about finding a pattern and making a rule:

No matter how many cards Emma has, James always has five more cards.

This problem tells you the rule: Emma's cards + 5 = James' cards.
If Emma has 15 cards, how many cards will James have?
James will have 15 + 5, or 20 cards.

Now see the same problem written a different way.

Emma's Cards Input (x)	James's Cards Output (y)
3	8
5	10
7	?
9	?

1. Identify the pattern: $3 + \underline{\ \ } = 8$
$5 + \underline{\ \ } = 10$
The pattern is **to add 5 to each number.**

2. Identify the rule and write it as an equation.
$x + 5 = y$
So the next numbers in the table are 12 and 14.

Write an equation that describes the pattern. Then use the equation to find the next three numbers in the pattern.

3.

Rule: _____	
Input (d)	Output (e)
4	8
8	12
12	
16	
20	

4.

Rule: _____	
Input (j)	Output (k)
2	11
5	14
8	
11	
14	

Name _____

Skills Practice

Function Tables: Find a Rule (+, −)

Write an equation that describes the pattern. Then use the equation to find the next three numbers in the pattern.

1.

Rule: _____	
Input (*a*)	Output (*b*)
0	2
5	7
10	
15	
20	

2.

Rule: _____	
Input (*f*)	Output (*g*)
22	17
26	21
30	
34	
38	

3.

Rule: _____	
Input (*h*)	Output (*j*)
12	19
15	22
18	
21	
24	

4.

Rule: _____	
Input (*t*)	Output (*u*)
25	14
29	18
33	
37	
41	

This table shows how much a drive-in movie theater charges.

Input (*p*)	Output (*t*)
2	9
3	10
4	
5	
6	

5. The drive-in movie theater charges $7 per car plus $1 per person. Use the table to the left to write an equation for this situation.

_____

6. Find the cost for bringing 4, 5, and 6 people to the movies.

_____

5-6

Reteach

Multiplication and Division Expressions

A variable is used in an expression to represent an unknown number. In the expression $5 \times x$, the unknown number is represented by the variable x.

You can find the value of an expression by substituting different numbers for the variable.

Find the value of $5 \times x$ if $x = 2$. $5 \times x$ $5 \times 2 = 10$ So, the value of $5 \times x$ if $x = 2$ is 10.	Find the value of $5 \times x$ when $x = 5$. $5 \times x$ $5 \times 5 = 25$ So, the value of $5 \times x$ when $x = 5$ is 25.
Find the value of $m \div 3$ when $m = 21$. $m \div 3$ $21 \div 3 = 7$ So, the value of $m \div 3$ when $m = 21$ is 7.	Find the value of $m \div 3$ if $m = 15$. $m \div 3$ $15 \div 3 = 5$ So, the value of $m \div 3$ if $m = 15$ is 5.

Find the value of the expression.

1. $m \times 1$ if $m = 1$ _____

3. $5 \times s$ when $s = 3$ _____

5. $16 \div y$ if $y = 2$ _____

7. $b \times 3$ when $b = 2$ _____

9. $c \times 4$ if $c = 5$ _____

11. $f \div 1$ when $f = 6$ _____

13. $a \div 2$ when $a = 8$ _____

15. $8 \times d$ when $d = 0$ _____

17. $3 \times x$ if $x = 4$ _____

19. $10 \div w$ if $w = 5$ _____

2. $z \times 4$ when $z = 10$ _____

4. $6 \times p$ if $p = 2$ _____

6. $30 \div l$ when $l = 6$ _____

8. $k \times 8$ when $k = 4$ _____

10. $r \div 6$ if $r = 48$ _____

12. $p \times 7$ if $p = 6$ _____

14. $g \div 3$ if $g = 21$ _____

16. $s \times 5$ when $s = 5$ _____

18. $n \times 9$ if $n = 3$ _____

20. $72 \div t$ when $t = 8$ _____

5-6

Skills Practice

Multiplication and Division Expressions

Find the value of each expression.

1. $3 \times (5 - 1)$ 2. $(7 \times 1) \div 2$ 3. $12 - (6 \div 2)$

_____   _____   _____

Circle the better expression.

4. Mark spent 10 minutes a day cleaning his room for 3 days and 15 minutes on the fourth day.

   A. $(10 \times 3) + 15$

   B. $10 \times (3 + 15)$

5. Jennifer had 20 stickers. She bought 10 more stickers. Then she gave half of her stickers to Melanie.

   F. $20 \times (10 \div 2)$

   G. $(20 \times 10) \div 2$

Find the value of each expression for the value given.

6. $(d \times 6) + 10$ for $d = 2$ _____

7. $8 + (5 \times z)$ for $z = 5$ _____

8. $(14 - n) \times 3$ for $n = 7$ _____

9. $(x + 2) \times 2$ for $x = 3$ _____

10. $x + (4 \times 5)$ for $x = 10$ _____

11. $8 - (15 \div x) \times 2$ for $x = 5$ _____

Solve. Use data from the chart for Exercises 12 and 13.

Item	Cost
pen	$3
ruler	$2
notebook	$4

12. Last week, Karla bought 3 pens and a ruler. How much did she spend?

_____

13. This week, all items are half price. How much will Karla pay for a ruler and a notebook? _____

Reteach

Problem-Solving Investigation: Choose a Strategy

There are many ways to solve most math problems. You will decide which strategy works best for you when you read the problems. Here is a list of problem-solving strategies:

- **Draw a picture:** This strategy can help you look at the information in the problem a different way—useful when the problem is about distance or location.

- **Look for a pattern:** This strategy can help you solve problems when the input changes.

- **Make a table:** This strategy can help you solve problems that have a lot of information to organize.

Use this problem to learn more about choosing a strategy.

When Lilly was 7 years old, she earned an allowance of 3 quarters. When she was 8 years old, she earned 5 quarters, and when she was 9 years old, she earned 7 quarters. Now Lilly is 10 years old. If the pattern continues how much allowance does Lilly earn?

Understand	You know that Lilly earned 3 quarters when she was 7, 5 quarters when she was 8, and 7 quarters when she was 9. You need to find how much allowance Lilly earns as a 10-year-old.
Plan	Choose a strategy. The input (Lilly's age) is changing. Looking for a pattern in the output (Lilly's allowance) will help you find the answer. Look for a pattern to solve this problem.

Name _____

Reteach

Problem-Solving Investigation (continued)

Solve	Age	7	8	9	10
	Allowance	3 quarters	5 quarters	7 quarters	?

Solve

Look at the three numbers. How do you get from 3 quarters to 5 quarters? How do you get from 5 quarters to 7 quarters? Is there a rule that tells how to get from one to another to the next?

Since the number of quarters is increasing, an amount is being added.

We can see that 5 is 2 higher than 3 so we know that 2 is being added.
To find the answer add 2 to 7. 2 quarters + 7 quarters is 9 quarters.

Check

Look back at the problem. Check that the difference between 9 quarters and 7 quarters is 2 quarters.
$9 - 7 = 2$
Your answer is correct.

Use any strategy on p. 38 to solve. Tell which strategy you used.

1. Each farmer brought 3 animals to the fair. If the fair has space in its barn for 84 animals, how many farmers can bring animals to

   the fair? _____

   Strategy: _____

2. Mackenzie is buying breakfast at school. Pancakes are $2, milk is $1, and eggs are $2. Mackenzie orders all three items. If she pays $7, how much change will she get back?

   _____

   Strategy: _____

5–7

Skills Practice

Problem-Solving Investigation: Choose a Strategy

Use any strategy shown below to solve. Tell which strategy you used.

- • Draw a picture
- • Make a table
- • Look for a pattern

1. When the new apartment building opened, 78 families moved in. If each family averaged 2 children, about how many children live

   in the new building? _____

   Strategy: _____

2. Luis spent $6 on groceries for his family. He bought eggs, milk, bananas, and bread. If he paid with a $20-bill, how much change

   did he get back? _____

   Strategy: _____

3. Olivia is making bead bracelets. She places two blue beads, then a green bead and a yellow bead. How many blue beads will she

   need if she uses 47 beads in all? _____

   Strategy: _____

4. Adam is helping his grandmother make a quilt. For every green square she uses, she needs 2 red squares, 3 yellow squares, and 4 white squares. If she uses 4 green squares, how many squares

   will she need in all? _____

   Strategy: _____

5. Madeline wants to download songs that cost $2 each. If she has

   $15, how many songs can she download? _____

   Strategy: _____

6. Erin picks up golf balls at the local golf course. Today she has collected 45 white balls, 17 yellow balls, 12 orange balls, and 5 pink balls. How many golf balls has Erin collected?

   _____

   _____

5-8

Reteach

Function Tables: Find a Rule (×, ÷)

Sometimes in math there is a pattern to the answers. Once you find the pattern, you can make a rule that will solve the problem for any input.

Use this problem to learn more about finding a pattern and making a rule.

> **No matter how many hats Vanessa has, Holly always has 4 times as many.**

This problem tells you the rule: Vanessa's hats × 4 = Holly's hats. If Vanessa has 5 hats, how many hats does Holly have?
Holly will have 5 × 4, or 20 hats.

Now see the same problem written a different way.

Rule: _____	
Vanessa's Hats Input (*v*)	Holly's Hats Output (*h*)
3	12
5	20
7	?
9	?

1. Identify the pattern: 3 × __ = 12
   5 × __ = 20
   The pattern is **to multiply each number by 4**.

2. Identify the rule and write it as an equation.
   $v \times 4 = h$
   So the next numbers in the table are 28 and 36.

Write an equation that describes the pattern. Then use the equation to find the next two numbers.

3.

Rule: _____	
Input (*d*)	Output (*e*)
1	3
2	6
3	9
4	
5	

4.

Rule: _____	
Input (*j*)	Output (*k*)
20	5
24	6
28	7
32	
36	

Name _____

Skills Practice

Function Tables: Find a Rule (×, ÷)

Write an equation that describes the pattern. Then use the equation to find the next two numbers.

1.

Rule: _____	
Input (f)	Output (g)
3	18
4	24
5	30
6	
7	

2.

Rule: _____	
Input (n)	Output (o)
27	3
36	4
45	5
54	
63	

3.

Rule: _____	
Input (h)	Output (i)
5	40
6	48
7	56
8	
9	

4.

Rule: _____	
Input (t)	Output (u)
7	1
14	2
21	3
28	
35	

5. My class has to form teams of five. Make a table to find how many teams we can make if there are 15, 20, 25, and 30 of us.

_____

Rule: _____	
Input (k)	Output (t)
15	
20	
25	
30	

Name _____ Date _____

Reteach

Multiples of 10, 100, and 1,000

Multiply each number below by 10 by adding a zero to the end of the number.

1. $2 \times 10 =$ _____

2. $3 \times 10 =$ _____

Multiply each number below by 100 by adding two zeros to the end of the number.

3. $7 \times 100 =$ _____

4. $1 \times 100 =$ _____

Multiply each number below by 1,000 by adding three zeros to the end of the number.

5. $6 \times 1,000 =$ _____

6. $9 \times 1,000 =$ _____

Multiply. Use basic facts and patterns.

7. $3 \times 5 = 15$

$3 \times 5\underline{0} = 15\underline{0}$

$3 \times 5\underline{00} =$ _____

$3 \times 5,\underline{000} = 15,\underline{000}$

8. $5 \times 2 =$ _____

$5 \times 2\underline{0} = 10\underline{0}$

$5 \times 2\underline{00} = 1,\underline{000}$

$5 \times 2,\underline{000} =$ _____

9. $4 \times 2 = 8$

$4 \times 2\underline{0} = 8\underline{0}$

$4 \times 2\underline{00} =$ _____

$4 \times 2,\underline{000} =$ _____

10. $6 \times 5 = 30$

$6 \times 5\underline{0} = 300\underline{0}$

$6 \times 5\underline{00} =$ _____

$6 \times 5,\underline{000} =$ _____

Multiply. Use mental math.

11. $1 \times 1,000 =$ _____

12. $6 \times 400 =$ _____

13. $9 \times 200 =$ _____

14. $8 \times 90 =$ _____

15. $3 \times 9,000 =$ _____

16. $2 \times 700 =$ _____

17. $5 \times 50 =$ _____

18. $4 \times 8,000 =$ _____

19. $8 \times 6,000 =$ _____

20. $7 \times 500 =$ _____

Name _____ Date _____

Skills Practice

Multiples of 10, 100, and 1,000

Multiply. Use basic facts and patterns.

1. $6 \times 30 =$ _____

2. $5 \times 300 =$ _____

3. $4 \times 3,000 =$ _____

4. $5 \times 40 =$ _____

5. $7 \times 300 =$ _____

6. $9 \times 1,000 =$ _____

7. $8 \times 20 =$ _____

8. $7 \times 500 =$ _____

9. $2 \times 9,000 =$ _____

10. $9 \times 80 =$ _____

11. $600 \times 5 =$ _____

12. $7,000 \times 4 =$ _____

13. $30 \times 2 =$ _____

14. $7 \times 200 =$ _____

15. $8 \times 700 =$ _____

16. $9 \times 700 =$ _____

17. $8 \times 50 =$ _____

18. $700 \times 6 =$ _____

19. $4,000 \times 9 =$ _____

20. $5 \times 60 =$ _____

Fine the value of each variable.

21. $5 \times n = 2,500$ _____

22. $8 \times n = 32,000$ _____

23. $1 \times n = 10$ _____

24. $60 \times n = 120$ _____

Reteach

Problem–Solving Skill: Reasonable Answers

Jeff wants to invite some friends over for dinner. He has a large rectangular table and knows there is room to seat 10 people on each of the long sides and 4 on the two ends of his table.

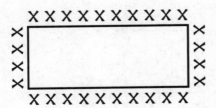

If Jeff wants everyone seated at the table, how many friends can he invite? Is it reasonable for him to invite 40 people?

Step 1: Understand. What facts do you know?   Jeff can seat 10 people on each of the long sides of his table.   Jeff can seat 4 people on each of the ends of his table.   Jeff wants everyone seated at the table.
Step 2: Plan. What you need to know?   How many friends is it reasonable for Jeff to invite?
Step 3: Solve. What math do you need to do?   You need to <u>figure out</u> the number of people that can sit at the table, based on all of the amounts that you have.   2 long sides, 10 people each: $10 \times 2 = 20$ 2 ends, 4 people each: $4 \times 2 = 8$ Add the amounts: $20 + 8 = 28$ people can sit at the table.
Step 4: Check. See if your answer makes sense.   When you <u>compare</u> the amount that can sit at the table, 28, to the amount of people that Jeff wants to invite, 40, you can see that it is not reasonable for him to invite 40 guests. If Jeff only has seats for 28, how many friends should he invite? (Remember, Jeff needs a seat too!)

Use the steps above to solve the following problem.

Brittany was given 3 movies to watch in her free time. Each movie is 100 minutes long. Brittany has 70 minutes to relax before she goes to work every day, Monday through Friday. Is it reasonable for her to expect to watch all three movies, starting Monday and ending on Friday?

Name _____ Date _____

Reteach (continued)

Problem–Solving Skill: Reasonable Answers

Step 1: Understand. What facts do you know?

_____

_____

_____

Step 2: Plan. What you need to know?

_____

_____

Step 3: Solve. What math do you need to do?

_____

_____

Figure out the total minutes it will take to watch all three movies.

_____

Step 4: Check. See if your answer makes sense.

_____

_____

_____

Decide whether each answer is reasonable. Explain your reasoning.

1. Sandy owns her own pizza restaurant. Her profit is about $2,000 a week. She needs to put aside $400 a week for taxes. Is it reasonable for her to spend $1,900 a week? _____

2. Sandy works 5 days a week. Her total number of hours each week is 50. Is it reasonable to say that Sandy works 7 hours a day?

_____

104

Name _____ Date _____

Skills Practice

Problem–Solving Skill: Reasonable Answers

Decide whether each answer is reasonable. Explain your reasoning.

1. Jill is in charge of the school fair that will go on for a week. There will be 10 different volunteers helping each day. Is 70 a reasonable estimate of the number of people who are expected to volunteer? _____

2. Jill will have to walk home from the fair each day for the week. The fair is 1 mile from her home. Is it reasonable to say that she will walk more than 10 miles before the week is over? _____

3. Jill expects that the sale of donated soda will bring in about $50 a day for the week. Is it reasonable for her to expect at least $500 from soda sales by the end of the week? _____

4. Jill was able to collect donations of about $60 a month for the 10 months that she was planning the fair. She saved all of the money. In addition, she was given $350 that had been put aside from the previous fair. She needs $1,000 to rent a ferris wheel. Is it reasonable to say that she can pay for the ferris wheel rental in full? _____

Types of Prizes	Number Collected
stuffed animals	98
plastic models	54
yo-yos	96
stopwatches	49

5. The table above shows the numbers of different prizes Jill collected for the fair. Is it reasonable for her to say that she has close to 300 prizes to give to those who win games?

_____

6. Jill has spent a total of 6,000 minutes organizing the fair. Is it reasonable for her to claim that she organized the fair in under 10 hours? _____

Name _____ Date _____

Reteach

Use Rounding to Estimate Products

To estimate products, round numbers. Then use basic facts and multiply.
Look at the number lines below.

Ones

$$\longleftarrow\!\!|\quad|\quad|\quad|\quad|\quad|\quad|\quad|\quad|\quad|\quad|\!\!\longrightarrow$$
  10 9 8 7 6 **5** 4 3 2 1 0

Tens

$$\longleftarrow\!\!|\quad|\quad|\quad|\quad|\quad|\quad|\quad|\quad|\quad|\quad|\!\!\longrightarrow$$
  10 20 30 40 50 60 70 80 90 100

Hundreds

$$\longleftarrow\!\!|\quad|\quad|\quad|\quad|\quad|\quad|\quad|\quad|\quad|\quad|\!\!\longrightarrow$$
  100 200 300 400 500 600 700 800 900 1,000

> Remember to round the greater factor to its greatest place.

When a number is halfway between two numbers, round up.

	Round the greater factor to its greatest place.	Use basic facts and multiply.
1. 59×5	_____	_____
2. 579×4	_____	_____
3. 788×3	_____	_____
4. $6,222 \times 6$	_____	_____
5. $8,951 \times 4$	_____	_____
6. 42×7	_____	_____
7. $6,450 \times 8$	_____	_____
8. 683×4	_____	_____
9. $7,395 \times 3$	_____	_____

107

Name _____ Date _____

Skills Practice

Use Rounding to Estimate Products

Estimate each product.

1. $5 \times 21 =$ _____

2. $3 \times 39 =$ _____

3. $7 \times \$46 =$ _____

4. $85 \times 6 =$ _____

5. $17 \times 9 =$ _____

6. $81 \times 3 =$ _____

7. $2 \times \$298 =$ _____

8. $4 \times 305 =$ _____

9. $478 \times 6 =$ _____

10. $5 \times 784 =$ _____

11. $612 \times 9 =$ _____

12. $6 \times 556 =$ _____

13. $2 \times 1,987 =$ _____

14. $3 \times \$2,126 =$ _____

15. $7 \times 1,905 =$ _____

16. $8 \times 3,495 =$ _____

17. $4,723 \times 4 =$ _____

18. $5 \times \$7,118 =$ _____

19. $41 \times 6 =$ _____

20. $28 \times 7 =$ _____

21. $96 \times 2 =$ _____

22. $17 \times 8 =$ _____

23. $31 \times 9 =$ _____

24. $255 \times 4 =$ _____

25. $488 \times 3 =$ _____

26. $563 \times 5 =$ _____

27. $2,307 \times 5 =$ _____

28. $7,596 \times 6 =$ _____

Solve.

29. The ambulance workers order 6 first aid kits. Each kit costs $39. About how much does it cost for 6 kits?

_____

30. An ambulance travels about 386 miles a day. About how many miles does it travel in a week?

_____

Name _____ Date _____

Reteach

Multiply Two-Digit Numbers

Find 13 × 3.

First, think in terms of tens and ones. 13 has 1 ten and 3 ones.

Second, set up the problem with the greater number on top.

13
×3

Solve the problem.

Step 1 **Multiply the ones.**	**Step 2** **Multiply the tens.**
13 3 × 3 = **9** ×3 —— **9** 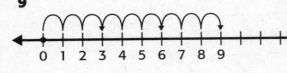 0 1 2 3 4 5 6 7 8 9	13 10 × 3 = **30** ×3 —— **39**  0 10 20 30 The tens (**30**) added to the ones (**9**) = **39**

Find 13 × 5.

First, think in terms of tens and ones. 13 has 1 ten and 3 ones.

Second, set up the problem with the greater number on top.

13
×5

Solve the problem.

Step 1 **Multiply the ones.**	**Step 2** **Multiply the tens. Add the new ten.**
13 3 × 5 = **15** ×5 —— **5** This time the product of the ones is larger. You need to regroup. You have 1 ten and 5 ones. **You need to add that ten to the other tens.**	1 13 10 × 5 = **50 + 10** ×5 —— **65** The tens (**50 + 10**) added to the ones (**5**) = **65**

Multiply. Check for reasonableness.

1. 26 × 5 = _____   **2.** 22 × 7 = _____   **3.** 45 × 3 = _____

Name _____ Date _____

Skills Practice

Multiply Two-Digit Numbers

Multiply. Check for reasonableness.

1. $21 \times 7 =$ _____

2. $38 \times 5 =$ _____

3. $54 \times 2 =$ _____

4. $49 \times 6 =$ _____

5. $17 \times 4 =$ _____

6. $25 \times 9 =$ _____

7. $53 \times 4 =$ _____

8. $28 \times 7 =$ _____

9. $61 \times 8 =$ _____

10. $39 \times 2 =$ _____

11. $62 \times 2 =$ _____

12. $38 \times 4 =$ _____

13. $91 \times 3 =$ _____

14. $46 \times 5 =$ _____

15. $78 \times 6 =$ _____

16. $98 \times 5 =$ _____

17. $76 \times 6 =$ _____

18. $24 \times 9 =$ _____

19. $56 \times 7 =$ _____

20. $48 \times 8 =$ _____

21. $66 \times 6 =$ _____

22. $77 \times 7 =$ _____

23. $94 \times 3 =$ _____

24. $59 \times 4 =$ _____

25. $44 \times 9 =$ _____

26. $24 \times 7 =$ _____

27. $19 \times 8 =$ _____

28. $67 \times 5 =$ _____

29. $84 \times 4 =$ _____

30. $91 \times 2 =$ _____

31. Look back over this page and circle every product greater than 300.

_____

6–5

Reteach

Problem-Solving Investigation: Choose a Strategy

Here are five problem-solving strategies and tips on how to use them.

Strategy	How to Use It
Use the four-step plan	Understand the facts. Plan your strategy. Solve the problem using the strategy. Check your work.
Draw a picture	Create a picture from the words in the problem to help you find the answer.
Look for a pattern	Spot whether there is something in the problem that repeats or looks the same.
Make a table	Organize data by making a table with columns for each category and rows for each number. Fill in the numbers to solve the problem.
Work backward	Start with the information given in the problem. Then use subtraction to find the answer to the problem.

Use any strategy shown below to solve. Tell what strategy you used.

- Use the four-step plan
- Draw a picture
- Look for a pattern
- Make a table
- Work backward

1. Bob wants to treat his 3 friends to rides at an amusement park. All-day passes cost $10. What will Bob have to pay for himself and his friends to go on the rides all day?

_____

Name _____ Date _____

Reteach (continued)

Problem-Solving Investigation: Choose a Strategy

2. Russ is setting up his science project about the seashore at the fair. He has several rocks at the edge of the water, on the right side of the display. He has sand on the left side. Five starfish are on the right side of the rocks, touching the water. Are the starfish next to the sand?

_____

_____

_____

3. Fill in the missing number. 3, 6, 12, 24, _____, 96, 192

_____

4. There are 5 marbles in each bag. How many marbles do you have if you are given 10 bags of red marbles, 12 bags of yellow marbles, and 8 bags of blue marbles?

_____

5. Mary now has 5 pairs of sneakers. Her friend gave her 1 white pair yesterday. Her mom bought her new pink ones this morning. How many pairs did she have originally?

_____

6. Hank is planting pepper plants. In the first row, he plants 1 pepper. In the second row, he plants 2. In the third row, he plants 4. In the fourth row he plants 8. How many peppers will he plant in the *sixth* row?

_____

7. Now, Jay has a collection of 20 baseball hats. He just got a new one on a school trip. Last week, his father's friend gave him 6 hats. How many hats did he have originally?

_____

8. Jerry was late to school all week. On Monday, Tuesday, and Wednesday; Jerry was 30 minutes late. On Thursday and Friday he was 50 minutes late. The principal told him that he would have to stay after school and make up all of the time before the end of the year. How many minutes will Jerry have to stay after school?

_____

Name _____ Date _____

Skills Practice

Problem-Solving Investigation: Choose a Strategy

Problem-Solving Strategies

- Draw a picture
- Look for a pattern
- Make a table
- Work backward

Use any strategy shown above to solve. Tell what strategy you used.

1. Fred is buying soda and snacks for a school event. He has to walk to the store and can only carry a limited amount at one time. He walked to the store 4 times. The first time he brought back 10 items, the second time 32, the third time 12, and the last time 15. How many items did he purchase?

   _____

2. Joe is building a storage shed. He needs 200 nails for each one of the 4 sides, 500 nails for the roof, 100 nails for the door, and 200 nails for the steps. How many nails will he need in all?

   _____

3. Andy is creating a design using colored shapes. He is starting with a triangle and ending with another triangle. In between the triangles, he has a circle to the left of a square. What does the design look like?

   _____

   _____

4. Gary rakes leaves. The first day, he fills 6 bags. The second day, he fills 8 bags. The third day, he fills 10 bags of leaves. If this pattern continues, how many bags will he fill on the fourth day?

   _____

5. Sherri now has 25 pairs of earrings. Last week she was given 2 pairs for her birthday. Just yesterday, her older sister gave her 2 sets of earrings. How many sets of earrings did she have originally?

   _____

Name _____ Date _____

Reteach

Multiply Multi-Digit Numbers

Multiply by following steps.

Find 22 × 6.

Step 1

Think in terms of tens and ones.
22 is 2 tens and 2 ones.

Tens	Ones
2	2

Step 2

Multiply the ones.

Tens	Ones
2	2

6

```
  1
 22        6
× 6      × 2     Regroup 12 ones as 1
        ————     ten + 2 ones. Be sure
          12     to put the 1 in the tens
                 column above the two.
```

Step 3

Multiply the tens.

Tens	Ones
2	2

6

```
   1
  22     6 × 2 tens = 12 tens. Add the regrouped ten.
 × 6     12 tens + 1 ten = 13 tens.
 ———
 132     Regroup 13 tens as 1 hundred and 3 tens.
```

Multiply.

1.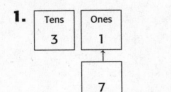

Tens	Ones
3	1

2.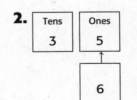

Tens	Ones
3	5

Name _____ Date _____

Skills Practice

Multiply Multi-Digit Numbers

Multiply. Check for reasonableness.

1. $114 \times 6 =$ _____

2. $261 \times 4 =$ _____

3. $628 \times 8 =$ _____

4. $739 \times 5 =$ _____

5. $295 \times 3 =$ _____

6. $375 \times 5 =$ _____

7. $648 \times 7 =$ _____

8. $31{,}525 \times 6 =$ _____

9. $11{,}313 \times 9 =$ _____

10. $24{,}512 \times 5 =$ _____

11. $16{,}421 \times 3 =$ _____

12. $\$1{,}225 \times 9 =$ _____

ALGEBRA Find the value of each expression if $t = 7$.

13. $t \times 385 =$ _____

14. $t \times 7{,}441 =$ _____

15. $t \times 91{,}123 =$ _____

Compare. Use >, <, or =.

16. 396×4 _____ 5×423

17. 4×712 _____ 3×412

18. 3×656 _____ 7×366

19. 6×523 _____ 2×379

20. 2×961 _____ 8×612

6–7

Reteach

Multiply Across Zeros

You can use the same steps to multiply numbers that contain zeros that you use to multiply any multidigit number.

Find 305×4.

Step 1	Step 2
Think in terms of hundreds, tens, and ones. 305 is 3 hundreds + 0 tens and 4 ones.	Multiply the **ones**. 2 305 $\underline{\times\ 4}\quad 4 \times 5 = 20$ Regroup 20 ones as 2 tens + $0\qquad\qquad$ 0 ones. Be sure to put the $\qquad\qquad\qquad$ 2 in the tens column above $\qquad\qquad\qquad$ the 0.
Step 3	**Step 4**
Multiply the **tens**. 2 305 $\underline{\times\ 4}\quad 4 \times 0 \text{ tens} = 0 \text{ tens}$ $20\quad$ Add the regrouped 2 tens. $\qquad\quad$ 0 tens + 2 tens = 2 tens	Multiply the **hundreds**. 2 305 $\underline{\times\ 4}\quad 4 \times 3 \text{ hundreds} = 1 \text{ thousand} +$ $1220\quad$ 2 hundreds. 0 ones + 2 tens + $\qquad\quad$ 2 hundreds + 1 thousand = 1220

Multiply. Check for reasonableness.

1. $402 \times 8 =$ _____

2. $7{,}009 \times 3 =$ _____

3. $5 \times 301 =$ _____

4. $6 \times 9{,}020 =$ _____

5. $2 \times 1{,}099 =$ _____

6. $7 \times 8{,}107 =$ _____

7. $806 \times 9 =$ _____

8. $5{,}007 \times 4 =$ _____

6-7

Skills Practice

Multiply Across Zeros

Multiply. Check for reasonableness.

1. 709 × 6 = _____

2. 450 × 3 = _____

3. 805 × 5 _____

4. 6,058 × 8 = _____

5. 5,608 × 4 = _____

6. 5,079 × 8 = _____

7. 1,047 × 7 = _____

8. 2,009 × 2 = _____

9. 4,010 × 3 = _____

10. 7,028 × 4 = _____

11. 5,001 × 9 = _____

12. 7,084 × 9 = _____

13. 4,807 × 7 = _____

14. 3,009 × 4 = _____

15. 9,012 × 6 = _____

16. 7,040 × 8 = _____

17. 1,027 × 5 = _____

18. 5,405 × 5 = _____

19. 3,004 × 3 = _____

20. 4,303 × 2 = _____

21. 1,009 × 3 = _____

22. 9,300 × 1 = _____

23. 9,099 × 9 = _____

Solve.

24. Tamara has 5 tall trees in her back yard. Each tree is 108 feet tall.

    How tall are all the trees put together?_____

25. Look back over the page and circle every product that has a 3 in the tens place. Draw a box around every product that has a 2 in the thousands place.

Name _____ Date _____

Reteach

Multiply by Tens

Find 355 × 40.

Step 1

Think in terms of hundreds, tens, and
ones. 355 = 3 hundreds + 5 tens + 5 ones.

$$\begin{array}{r} 355 \\ \times\ 40 \\ \hline \end{array}$$

	Tens	Ones
	5	5

Step 2

Multiply the ones.

$$\begin{array}{r} 355 \\ \uparrow \\ \times\ 40 \\ \hline 0 \end{array}$$ 0 × (any number) 355 = 0

Step 3

Multiply the tens × the ones.

$$\begin{array}{r} 2 \\ 355 \\ \uparrow \\ \times\ 40 \\ \hline 00 \end{array}$$ 4 × 5 ones = 20 ones

Add the regrouped 2 tens.

Step 4

Multiply the tens × the tens.

$$\begin{array}{r} 22 \\ 355 \\ \uparrow \\ \times\ 40 \\ \hline 200 \end{array}$$ 4 × 5 tens = 20 tens + 2 tens

Add the regrouped 200

Step 5

Multiply the tens × the hundreds.

$$\begin{array}{r} 22 \\ 355 \\ \uparrow \\ \times\ 40 \\ \hline 14200 \end{array}$$ 4 × 3 hundreds = 12 hundreds +
2 hundreds. Add the regrouped 200

Multiply.

1. 44 × 20 _____

2. 658 × 30 _____

Name _____ Date _____

Skills Practice

Multiply by Tens

Multiply.

1. $12 \times 30 =$ _____

2. $21 \times 40 =$ _____

3. $14 \times 60 =$ _____

4. $31 \times 70 =$ _____

5. $25 \times 50 =$ _____

6. $24 \times 40 =$ _____

7. $61 \times 30 =$ _____

8. $48 \times 20 =$ _____

9. $19 \times 30 =$ _____

10. $65 \times 40 =$ _____

11. $48 \times 40 =$ _____

12. $14 \times 50 =$ _____

13. $49 \times 70 =$ _____

14. $42 \times 90 =$ _____

15. $80 \times 7 =$ _____

16. $26 \times 40 =$ _____

17. $17 \times 80 =$ _____

18. $135 \times 50 =$ _____

19. $207 \times 60 =$ _____

20. $399 \times 50 =$ _____

21. $756 \times 30 =$ _____

22. $2{,}375 \times 20 =$ _____

23. $4{,}009 \times 40 =$ _____

24. $2{,}490 \times 70 =$ _____

25. $6{,}967 \times 10 =$ _____

26. $9{,}075 \times 80 =$ _____

27. $5{,}549 \times 50 =$ _____

28. $1{,}005 \times 30 =$ _____

Solve.

29. Classroom chairs cost $39. How much will it cost to buy 30 chairs?

_____

30. A computer costs $986. How much will it cost to buy
20 computers?

_____

Name _____ Date _____

Reteach

Multiply by Tens

Find 355 × 40.

Step 1

Think in terms of hundreds, tens, and ones. 355 = 3 hundreds + 5 tens + 5 ones.

```
 355
× 40
```

	Tens	Ones
	5	5

Step 2

Multiply the ones.

```
   355
    ↑
×  40   0 × (any number) 355 = 0
─────
    0
```

Step 3

Multiply the tens × the ones.

```
    2
  355
    ↑
× 40   4 × 5 ones = 20 ones
────
  00   Add the regrouped 2 tens.
```

Step 4

Multiply the tens × the tens.

```
  22
 355
   ↑
× 40   4 × 5 tens = 20 tens + 2 tens
─────
 200   Add the regrouped 200
```

Step 5

Multiply the tens × the hundreds.

```
   22
  355
    ↑
×  40   4 × 3 hundreds = 12 hundreds +
──────
14200   2 hundreds. Add the regrouped 200
```

Multiply.

1. 44 × 20 _____

2. 658 × 30 _____

Name _____ Date _____

Skills Practice

Multiply by Tens

Multiply.

1. $12 \times 30 =$ _____

2. $21 \times 40 =$ _____

3. $14 \times 60 =$ _____

4. $31 \times 70 =$ _____

5. $25 \times 50 =$ _____

6. $24 \times 40 =$ _____

7. $61 \times 30 =$ _____

8. $48 \times 20 =$ _____

9. $19 \times 30 =$ _____

10. $65 \times 40 =$ _____

11. $48 \times 40 =$ _____

12. $14 \times 50 =$ _____

13. $49 \times 70 =$ _____

14. $42 \times 90 =$ _____

15. $80 \times 7 =$ _____

16. $26 \times 40 =$ _____

17. $17 \times 80 =$ _____

18. $135 \times 50 =$ _____

19. $207 \times 60 =$ _____

20. $399 \times 50 =$ _____

21. $756 \times 30 =$ _____

22. $2{,}375 \times 20 =$ _____

23. $4{,}009 \times 40 =$ _____

24. $2{,}490 \times 70 =$ _____

25. $6{,}967 \times 10 =$ _____

26. $9{,}075 \times 80 =$ _____

27. $5{,}549 \times 50 =$ _____

28. $1{,}005 \times 30 =$ _____

Solve.

29. Classroom chairs cost \$39. How much will it cost to buy 30 chairs?

_____

30. A computer costs \$986. How much will it cost to buy 20 computers?

_____

Name _____ Date _____

Reteach

Estimate Products

You can round to estimate products. Round each factor to its greatest place. Then multiply using patterns with zeros.

Estimate 42 × 59.

42 →	40	1 zero
× 59 →	× 60	× 1 zero
	2,400	2 zeros

Estimate 74 × 229.

229 →	200	2 zeros
× 74 →	× 70	× 1 zero
	14,000	3 zeros

Estimate each product by rounding.

1. 54 →
    × 19 → _____

2. $29 →
    × 32 → _____

3. 788 →
    × 51 → _____

Estimate each product.

4. 37 × 49 _____

5. 23 × 51 _____

6. 69 × 19 _____

7. 26 × $72 _____

8. 19 × 315 _____

9. 85 × 263 _____

10. 72 × 803 _____

11. 48 × 1,056 _____

12. 92 × 2,228 _____

Name _____ Date _____

Skills Practice

Estimate Products

Estimate each product.

1. 49 × 59 _____
2. 85 × 1,211 _____
3. 55 × 65 _____
4. 71 × 2,118 _____
5. 41 × 52 _____
6. 19 × 6,302 _____
7. 18 × 29 _____
8. 29 × 7,907 _____
9. 98 × 402 _____
10. 98 × 3,010 _____
11. 71 × 874 _____
12. 37 × 8,196 _____
13. 61 × $216 _____
14. 42 × 3,284 _____
15. 81 × 350 _____
16. 4,980 × 16 _____
17. 42 × 605 _____
18. 4,230 × 21 _____
19. 23 × 999 _____
20. 5,890 × 36 _____

Solve by estimating each product.

21. The price of a bus ticket is $58. About how much will tickets cost for a group of 62 passengers? _____

22. An airline ticket costs $375. About how much will tickets cost for a group of 25 people? _____

23. Michael averages 12 points in each football game. About how many points will he score in 12 games? _____

24. Rachel creates 14 paintings a month. About how many paintings will she create in 2 years? _____

7–3

Reteach

Problem-Solving Strategy: Act It Out

Yolan has 3 bills equaling $20. What combination of $1, $5, $10, $20, or $50 bills does he have?

Understand	Be sure you understand the problem. What do you know? • Yolan has 3 bills. • The value of those bills is $20. What do you need to find? • You need to find what bills Yolan has.
Plan	Make a plan. You can act out the problem using play money.
Solve	Use play money to act out different combinations of $20. Cut out pieces of paper to represent different amounts of money. Try out different possibilities with the bills. He could have two $5 bills and one $10 bill.
Check	Is the solution reasonable? Reread the problem. Check your answer.

Solve. Use the act it out strategy.

1. Rod has 20 coins having the value of $6. What coins does he have?

_____

2. List 3 combinations to create a value of 64 cents.

_____

_____

3. Angie is 8 years old. She is one-fifth her father's age. How old is her father?

_____

Name _____ Date _____

Reteach

Problem-Solving Strategy (continued)

4. You decide to start a business making T-shirts with Joe, Frank, and Eddie. In one day Joe created 6 more than Frank. Frank created 4 less than Eddie. On that day, the total number of T-shirts the boys created was 22. How many shirts did each boy create?

_____

5. The boys have $100 to spend. They have a total of four $5, $10, $20, or $50 bills. What combination of bills do they have?

_____

6. There are 10 people interested in buying shirts. All 10 people unfold and inspect the 22 shirts. After each person unfolds a shirt, Frank folded it again. How many times did Frank refold shirts?

_____

7. After selling shirts, the boys had $500 in cash. They had a total of 19 bills. What combination of bills did they have?

_____

8. Eddie figured out that he could cut a large square of fabric into 4 small squares, and each small square was enough for 1 T-shirt. In the end, the boys ruined 2 shirts and had 22 good ones. How many large squares of fabric did they start with?

_____

9. Leah is 13 years older than Jillian. Jillian is 2 years younger than Steve. If Steve is 11, how old is Leah?

_____

Name _____ Date _____

Skills Practice

Problem-Solving Strategy: Act It Out

Solve. Use the act it out strategy.

1. Ann is 50. Ann is twice the age of her daughter, Cindy. Cindy's daughter is 20 years younger than her mother. How old is Cindy's daughter?

_____

2. Jane is 64 years old and 4 years older than 3 times Linda's age. How old is Linda?

_____

3. Jerry has 12 bills equaling $100. ($5, $10, $20, $50) What combination of bills does he have?

_____

_____

4. Fred has 34 coins equaling $3. What combination of coins does he have?

_____

5. The Gomez family goes to a symphony concert. They buy 1 adult ticket at $15 and 3 youth tickets at $9. How much does the Gomez family spend for tickets?

_____

6. There are 30 students in the lunch line. On the shelf there are an equal number of 5 different kinds of drinks. If there are 30 drinks on the shelf, how many people have the same kind of drink?

_____

Reteach

Multiply Two-Digit Numbers

Find 36 × 26.
Estimate: 40 × 30 = 1,200

Step 1 Multiply the ones. Regroup if necessary. Cross out the amount you regroup when you add it.

```
    3
    3  6
 ×  2  6
 2  1  6
```

Step 2 Multiply the tens. Regroup if necessary. Cross out the amount you regroup when you add it. Remember, a zero is in the ones place when you multiply the tens.

```
 1  3
    3  6
 ×  2  6
 2  1  6        6 × 3  6
 7  2  0        2 × 3  6
```

Step 3 Add.

```
 1  3
    3  6
 ×  2  6
 2  1  6        6 × 3  6
 7  2  0        2 × 3  6
 9  3  6
```

Multiply.

1. 14 × 22 _____   **2.**   30 × 13 _____

3. 42 × 17 _____   **4.**   30 × 24 _____

Name _____ Date _____

Skills Practice

Multiply Two-Digit Numbers

Use models on graph paper to help you multiply. You may need to tape grids together.

1. $13 \times 22 =$ _____ **2.** $17 \times 21 =$ _____ **3.** $25 \times 24 =$ _____

4. $43 \times 15 =$ _____ **5.** $31 \times 18 =$ _____ **6.** $20 \times 19 =$ _____

Multiply.

7. $\begin{array}{r} 36 \\ \times\ 12 \\ \hline \end{array}$ **8.** $\begin{array}{r} 45 \\ \times\ 35 \\ \hline \end{array}$ **9.** $\begin{array}{r} 31 \\ \times\ 25 \\ \hline \end{array}$

10. $\begin{array}{r} 27 \\ \times\ 41 \\ \hline \end{array}$ **11.** $\begin{array}{r} 48 \\ \times\ 20 \\ \hline \end{array}$ **12.** $\begin{array}{r} 12 \\ \times\ 46 \\ \hline \end{array}$

13. $\begin{array}{r} 38 \\ \times\ 14 \\ \hline \end{array}$ **14.** $\begin{array}{r} 38 \\ \times\ 27 \\ \hline \end{array}$ **15.** $\begin{array}{r} 36 \\ \times\ 36 \\ \hline \end{array}$

16. $\begin{array}{r} 23 \\ \times\ 22 \\ \hline \end{array}$ **17.** $\begin{array}{r} 32 \\ \times\ 15 \\ \hline \end{array}$ **18.** $\begin{array}{r} 28 \\ \times\ 44 \\ \hline \end{array}$

19. $\begin{array}{r} 49 \\ \times\ 13 \\ \hline \end{array}$ **20.** $\begin{array}{r} 45 \\ \times\ 25 \\ \hline \end{array}$ **21.** $\begin{array}{r} 16 \\ \times\ 40 \\ \hline \end{array}$

22. $\begin{array}{r} 47 \\ \times\ 34 \\ \hline \end{array}$ **23.** $\begin{array}{r} 14 \\ \times\ 15 \\ \hline \end{array}$ **24.** $\begin{array}{r} 17 \\ \times\ 17 \\ \hline \end{array}$

25. $\begin{array}{r} 46 \\ \times\ 14 \\ \hline \end{array}$ **26.** $\begin{array}{r} 26 \\ \times\ 34 \\ \hline \end{array}$ **27.** $\begin{array}{r} 37 \\ \times\ 26 \\ \hline \end{array}$

28. $\begin{array}{r} 17 \\ \times\ 25 \\ \hline \end{array}$ **29.** $\begin{array}{r} 32 \\ \times\ 18 \\ \hline \end{array}$ **30.** $\begin{array}{r} 19 \\ \times\ 27 \\ \hline \end{array}$

Name _____ Date _____

Reteach

Multiply Three-Digit Numbers by Two-Digit Numbers

Find 411 × 12.   Estimate: 400 × 10 = 4,000

Step 1   **Multiply the ones.** 411 × 2

$$\begin{array}{r} 411 \\ \times 12 \\ \hline 822 \end{array}$$

Step 2   **Multiply the tens.** 411 × 10
Remember, a zero is in the ones place when you multiply the tens.

$$\begin{array}{r} 411 \\ \times 12 \\ \hline 822 \\ \mathbf{4110} \end{array}$$

Step 3   **Add the products.** 822 + 4110

$$\begin{array}{r} 411 \\ \times 12 \\ \hline 822 \\ 4110 \\ \hline \mathbf{4,932} \end{array}$$

Solve.

1. 419 × 24 _____

2. 553 × 36 _____

3. 245 × 26 _____

4. 339 × 74 _____

5. 153 × 75 _____

6. 414 × 48 _____

7. 463 × 22 _____

8. 202 × 23 _____

9. 218 × 90 _____

10. 186 × 80 _____

11. 350 × 61 _____

12. 727 × 31 _____

13. 247 × 35 _____

14. 643 × 57 _____

15. 668 × 44 _____

16. 915 × 29 _____

Name _____ Date _____

Skills Practice

Multiply Three-Digit Numbers by Two-Digit Numbers

Multiply.

1. 869 × 59 _____

2. 357 × 16 _____

3. 359 × 10 _____

4. 981 × 53 _____

5. 456 × 38 _____

6. 523 × 26 _____

7. 309 × 19 _____

8. 500 × 20 _____

9. 296 × 33 _____

10. 198 × 41 _____

11. 302 × 11 _____

12. 517 × 68 _____

13. 775 × 19 _____

14. 120 × 42 _____

15. 343 × 59 _____

16. 118 × 13 _____

17. 296 × 21 _____

18. 178 × 12 _____

19. 373 × 14 _____

20. 385 × 15 _____

Solve.

21. Ali's mom said for every 20 hours Ali worked, she would earn $150.

After Ali worked 40 hours, how much did she earn? _____

22. Patti's heart beats 125 times in a minute. How many times does

her heart beat in an hour? _____

7-6

Reteach

Problem-Solving Investigation: Choose a Strategy

Mandy went shopping. Her mother gave her a bank card to use and told her that she could not spend more than $200. Mandy spent $56 in the first store, $87 in the next, then $95, and finally $103. When she got home, Mandy told her mother that she wasn't sure but thought she stayed under $200. Does this make mathematical sense?

Understand	**Be sure you understand the problem.** What do you know? • Mandy has a limit of $200. • She spent $56, $87, $95, and $103. What do you need to find? • You need to find if Mandy stayed within her limit.
Plan	**Make a plan.** You can use the make a table strategy to find how much Mandy spent. You can estimate the amount Mandy spent at each store and place the amounts in the table. <table><tr><th>Store #1</th><th>Store #2</th><th>Store #3</th><th>Store #4</th></tr><tr><td>$56</td><td>$87</td><td>$95</td><td>$103</td></tr></table>
Solve	$56 + $87 + $95 + $103 = $341 $341 − $200 = $141 So, Mandy spent $141 over her $200 limit.
Check	**Is the solution reasonable?** Reread the problem. Check your answer.

Solve and tell what strategies you used.

1. Sandy spent $459 on gifts. She spent about $50 on each person. How many people did she buy gifts for?

_____

Name _____ Date _____

Reteach (continued)

Problem-Solving Investigation: Choose a Strategy

2. Caitlin, Erin, and Jeannie are on the track team. Over the season, Caitlin won 2 times and came in second 2 times. Erin won 1 time and came in second 5 times. Jeannie did not win at all, but came in second 8 times. The runners earn 10 points for winning and 5 points for coming in second. Who got the most points this season?

_____

3. Kyle is 4,000 days old. About how many years old is he?

_____

4. Hao solved the following problem.
   $42 \times 37 = 1,554$
   Explain how Hao could check his answer.

_____

_____

_____

5. Victoria has 12 photo albums to make gifts for her family. Each photo album will need $0.30 of buttons and $1 of ribbon. She estimates she will spend $15. Did she overestimate or underestimate?

_____

_____

6. Carmen bought 5 dozen muffins for her class. Each student got 2 muffins. Estimate how many people are in Carmen's class and explain your answer.

_____

7. Every teacher at Mountain Elementary is provided 4,000 sheets of paper. How many sheets of paper do the 50 teachers have altogether?

_____

8. Isra is thinking of two numbers that have a sum of 7 and a product of 10. What are the two numbers?

_____

7-6

Skills Practice

Problem-Solving Investigation: Choose a Strategy

Use any strategy to solve. Tell what strategy you used.

- Make a table
- Work backward
- Choose an operation
- Act it out

1. Beth bought 4 boxes of beads. Each box held 305 beads. How

   many beads did she buy in all? _____ beads
   Tell which strategy you used.

   _____

2. Each box of beads cost $2. Beth bought 6 boxes. How much

   did she spend on all of the beads? $ _____
   Tell which strategy you used.

   _____

3. Brian and Gaby are decorating boxes with beads for the craft fair.
   Each box uses 705 beads. How many beads do they need to

   decorate 4 boxes? _____ beads
   Tell which strategy you used.

   _____

4. Brian and Gaby sell each decorated box for $15. If they sell

   3 boxes, how much money will they make? $ _____
   Tell which strategy you used.

   _____

5. For the 10-kilometer race, there were 698 runners. Each runner
   was given 3 passes for friends and family to be at the finish line.

   How many passes were given out? _____ passes
   Tell which strategy you used.

   _____

6. Runners paid $6 to enter the race. How much money was

   collected from 437 runners? $ _____
   Tell which strategy you used.

   _____

Reteach

Multiply Greater Numbers

Find $4,263 \times 43$.
Estimate: $4,000 \times 40 = 160,000$

Step 1 Multiply the ones. Regroup if necessary. Cross out the amount you regroup when you add it.

```
    1
  4,263
 ×   43
 ──────
 12,789        4,263 × 3
 ──────
```

Step 2 Multiply the tens. Remember, a zero is in the ones place when you multiply the tens.

```
  1 2 1
    1
  4,263
 ×   43
 ──────
 12,789        4,263 × 3
 ──────
 170,520       4,263 × 40
```

Step 3 Add.

```
  1 2 1
    1
  4,263
 ×   43
 ──────
 12,789        4,263 × 3
 ──────
 170,520       4,263 × 40
 ───────
 183,309
```

Multiply.

1. $1,435 \times 45$ _____

2. $6,901 \times 38$ _____

3. $7,468 \times 31$ _____

4. $5,297 \times 12$ _____

5. $5,852 \times 52$ _____

6. $8,448 \times 24$ _____

Name _____ Date _____

Skills Practice
Multiply Greater Numbers

Multiply.

1. 693
   × 4

2. $601
   × 3

3. 8,072
   × 8

4. 907
   × 5

5. 2,901
   × 2

6. $38.88
   × 4

7. 6 × 2,369 = _____

8. 9 × $1,288 = _____

9. 5 × 19,091 = _____

10. 8 × 12,967 = _____

11. Multiply 3,687 by 8. _____

12. Multiply 1,096 by 9. _____

ALGEBRA Complete the table.

13.

Input	12	15	18	21	24
Output	48	60			

14.

Input	1	2	3	4	5
Output	37	74			

Solve.

15. Maria made 9 trips between New York City and Los Angeles. Each trip cost $498. How much did the 9 trips cost? _____

16. A company buys 8 computers. Each computer costs $2,245. How much does the company spend on the 8 computers? _____

8-1

Reteach

Division with Remainders

Interpret the Remainder

There are 26 people seated at tables. Each table seats 8 people. How many full tables are there? How many people are sitting at a table that is not full? How many tables are needed for all 26 people?

There are 3 different ways to interpret the remainder.

1. Use only the quotient. How many full tables will there be?	Divide to find the number of full tables. $26 \div 8 = $ **3** R2 There will be 3 full tables.
2. The remainder is the answer. How many people will sit at a table that is not full?	Look at the remainder. $26 \div 8 = 3$ **R2** So, 2 people will sit at a table that is not full.
3. Add 1 to the quotient. How many tables will be needed for all 26 people?	Since there are 3 full tables and 1 table that is not full, there are 4 tables in all.

Choose the correct answer.

There are 94 people who volunteer to clean the park. They will form into groups of 4. How many groups of 4 can they make?

1. Which of the following statements is true?

    A They will make 24 groups.
    B Everyone can be in a group of 4.
    C There are 98 volunteers.

Divide. Check each answer.

2. $17 \div 4 = $ _____   **3.** $43 \div 5 = $ _____   **4.** $9 \div 2 = $ _____

5. $27 \div 5 = $ _____   **6.** $57 \div 9 = $ _____   **7.** $21 \div 4 = $ _____

Name _____ Date _____

Skills Practice

Division with Remainders

Divide. Check each answer.

1. $8\overline{)91}$ _____

2. $3\overline{)54}$ _____

3. $9\overline{)16}$ _____

4. $5\overline{)86}$ _____

5. $7\overline{)12}$ _____

6. $7\overline{)21}$ _____

7. $3\overline{)24}$ _____

8. $4\overline{)36}$ _____

9. $7\overline{)43}$ _____

10. $5\overline{)26}$ _____

11. $6\overline{)89}$ _____

12. $4\overline{)17}$ _____

13. $3\overline{)94}$ _____

14. $4\overline{)21}$ _____

15. $23 \div 2 =$ _____

16. $35 \div 7 =$ _____

17. $27 \div 3 =$ _____

18. $19 \div 9 =$ _____

19. $24 \div 7 =$ _____

20. $38 \div 6 =$ _____

Name _____ Date _____

Reteach

Divide Multiples of 10, 100, and 1,000

You can use patterns or basic facts to help you divide multiples of 10, 100, and 1,000.

You need to find 1,800 ÷ 6.

Use a Multiplication Pattern	Use a Basic Fact
Think $6 \times ? = 1,800$	Think. What is the basic fact?
$6 \times 3 = 18 \quad \rightarrow \quad 18 \div 6 = 3$	The basic fact for $1,800 \div 6$ is $18 \div 6$.
$6 \times 30 = 180 \quad \rightarrow \quad 180 \div 6 = 30$	$18 \div 6 = 3$
$6 \times 300 = 1,800 \rightarrow 1,800 \div 6 = 300$	$180 \div 6 = 30$
	$1,800 \div 6 = 300$

Complete each set of patterns.

1. $15 \div 3 =$ _____

  $150 \div 3 =$ _____

  $1,500 \div 3 =$ _____

2. $63 \div 9 =$ _____

  $630 \div 9 =$ _____

  $6,300 \div 9 =$ _____

3. $30 \div 5 =$ _____

  $300 \div 5 =$ _____

  $3,000 \div 5 =$ _____

4. $32 \div 8 =$ _____

  $320 \div 8 =$ _____

  $3,200 \div 8 =$ _____

Divide. Use patterns.

5. $800 \div 2 =$ _____

6. $4,200 \div 7 =$ _____

7. $270 \div 9 =$ _____

8. $600 \div 3 =$ _____

9. $150 \div 5 =$ _____

Name _____ Date _____

Skills Practice

Divide Multiples of 10, 100, and 1,000

Divide. Use Patterns.

1. $200 \div 5 =$ _____

2. $4,500 \div 9 =$ _____

3. $5,400 \div 9 =$ _____

4. $\$3,500 \div 7 =$ _____

5. $\$8,100 \div 9 =$ _____

6. $900 \div 3 =$ _____

7. $54 \div 9 =$ _____

8. $6,400 \div 8 =$ _____

9. $6,400 \div 8 =$ _____

10. $4,200 \div 6 =$ _____

Complete each set of patterns.

11. $18 \div 3 =$ _____

12. $63 \div 7 =$ _____

    $180 \div 3 =$ _____

    $630 \div 7 =$ _____

    $1,800 \div 3 =$ _____

    $6,300 \div 7 =$ _____

13. $30 \div 6 =$ _____

14. $42 \div 7 =$ _____

    $300 \div 6 =$ _____

    $420 \div 7 =$ _____

    $3,000 \div 6 =$ _____

    $4,200 \div 7 =$ _____

15. $25 \div 5 =$ _____

16. $21 \div 3 =$ _____

    $250 \div 5 =$ _____

    $210 \div 3 =$ _____

    $2,500 \div 5 =$ _____

    $2,100 \div 3 =$ _____

Problem Solving.

17. Sam has 720 toothpicks in packages. Each package has 90 toothpicks. How many packages of toothpicks does Sam have?

_____

18. The Harris family went on a vacation. They traveled 630 miles in 7 days. How many miles did they travel each day?

_____

8–3

Reteach

Problem-Solving Strategy: Guess and Check

Solve problems using the guess and check strategy.

Jenny fills a bottle with 8 inches of colored sand. She has 2 inches more of red sand than of blue sand. How many inches of each color does she use?

Step 1. Understand	**Be sure you understand the problem.** Read carefully. What do you know? • Jenny's bottle holds ____ inches of sand. • There are _____ of red sand than of blue sand What do you need to find? • You need to find how many _____ _____
Step 2. Plan	**Make a plan.** • Use the guess and check strategy. • List the information you know. • Use what you know to make a guess. • Guess how many inches of each color sand are needed to make a total of 8 inches. • Check your guess. • Revise the guess and try again if it is wrong. • Guess, check, and revise until you find the answer that makes sense.

8-3

Reteach

Problem-Solving Strategy (continued)

Step 3. Solve	**Carry out your plan.**
	You know that the bottle holds _____ inches of sand.
	You know that Jenny has _____ more
	inches of _____ sand than of _____ sand.
	Guess Start with two numbers that have a sum of 8. Try 6 and 2.
	Check 6 + 2 = 8
	_____ inches of red sand, _____ inches of blue sand
	There are _____ more inches of red sand.
	Does that answer fit the problem? _____
	Revise 5 + 3 = 8
	_____ inches of red sand, _____ inches of blue sand
	There are _____ more inches of red sand.
	Does that answer fit the problem? _____
Step 4. Check	**Is the solution reasonable?** Reread the problem.
	Does your answer make all of the statements true?
	_____

Practice

1. A group of friends share 30 stickers equally, with 3 stickers left over. There are more than 5 friends. How many friends are there? How many stickers does each friend get?

   _____

2. Erica invites 8 friends to her party. She wants each friend to have 3 balloons. She has 27 balloons. How many balloons

   will she have left over? _____

8-3

Skills Practice

Problem-Solving Strategy: Guess and Check

Solve. Use the guess and check strategy.

1. Teri puts 57 dolls in a display case. She puts the same number on each shelf and has 3 dolls left. The case has more than 7 shelves. How many shelves does the case have? How many dolls does

   each shelf hold? _____

2. A group of friends choose cards equally from a deck of 52 cards. There are more than 6 friends. After they have chosen, 4 cards are left. How many friends are there? How many cards does each

   friend have? _____

3. Jamal buys 59 stickers. Stickers come in packs of 5 or 8. How many packs of 5 stickers does Jamal buy? 8 stickers?

   _____

4. There are 36 students in an auditorium. There are twice as many girls as boys. How many girls are there? How many boys are there?

   _____

5. Chou makes a display. He puts 1 photo in the first row, 4 photos in the second row, 7 in the third row, and 10 in the fourth row. If the pattern continues, how many photos does Chou put in the

   fifth row? _____

6. Each of the 50 states in the United States has a state flag. Evelyn wants to make a drawing of each state flag. She has 3 more flags

   to draw. How many flags has Evelyn drawn? _____

7. Sally wants to arrive 20 minutes early for her job. She starts work at 4:15 P.M. It will take her about 20 minutes to walk from school

   to the job. When should Sally leave? _____

8. Create a problem that can be solved by using the guess-and-check

   strategy. Share it with others. _____

Reteach

Estimate Quotients

Compatible numbers are numbers you can divide easily.
You can use compatible numbers to estimate quotients.

Estimate 3,463 ÷ 7.

3,463 ÷ **7**   Think: A basic fact that is close is 35 ÷ 7.

3,500 ÷ 7 = 500

So, 3,463 ÷ 7 is about 500.

Complete.

1. Estimate 1,785 ÷ 3.

Division fact: 18 ÷ 3 = ___

Estimate: 1,800 ÷ 3 = _____

2. Estimate 2,880 ÷ 3.

Division fact: 27 ÷ 3 = ___

Estimate: 2,700 ÷ 3 = _____

3. Estimate 5,726 ÷ 7.

Division fact: _____

Estimate: _____

4. Estimate 3,952 ÷ 8.

Division fact: _____

Estimate: _____

Estimate. Check your estimate.

5. 1,482 ÷ 3 _____

6. 6,512 ÷ 8 _____

7. 7,164 ÷ 9 _____

8. 2,207 ÷ 7 _____

9. 3,512 ÷ 4 _____

10. 2,587 ÷ 5 _____

11. 3,123 ÷ 6 _____

12. 4,132 ÷ 7 _____

13. 2,712 ÷ 3 _____

14. 1,789 ÷ 3 _____

15. 2,797 ÷ 4 _____

16. 6,432 ÷ 9 _____

Name _____ Date _____

Skills Practice
Estimate Quotients

Estimate. Check your estimate.

1. $2\overline{)43}$

2. $2\overline{)71}$

3. $6\overline{)521}$

4. $7\overline{)501}$

5. $2\overline{)131}$

6. $9\overline{)286}$

7. $8\overline{)650}$

8. $5\overline{)209}$

9. $6\overline{)3,124}$

10. $4\overline{)3,105}$

11. $3\overline{)5,896}$

12. $9\overline{)4,699}$

13. $65 \div 3$ _____

14. $98 \div 5$ _____

15. $22 \div 3$ _____

16. $381 \div 8$ _____

17. $555 \div 6$ _____

18. $640 \div 7$ _____

19. $4,124 \div 6$ _____

20. $1,912 \div 9$ _____

21. $1,714 \div 2$ _____

22. $2,186 \div 4$ _____

23. $2,904 \div 7$ _____

24. $4,711 \div 8$ _____

Solve.

25. Marta travels a total of 850 miles every month to San Francisco on business. If she goes 3 times a month, about how many miles is each round trip?

_____

26. Jeff goes on a 173-mile bike trip. It takes him 9 days from start to finish. About how many miles does he travel each day?

_____

Name _____ Date _____

Reteach

Two-Digit Quotients

Tens	Ones
5	3

53 ÷ 2 is 53 divided in 2 parts.

Step 1 Set up the problem with the number being divided
$2\overline{)53}$ on the inside and the divisor on the outside.

Step 2 Divide the tens and write the amount in the tens box.
Then, subtract.

$$\begin{array}{r} 2 \\ 2\overline{)53} \\ -4 \\ \hline 1 \end{array}$$

Divide the 5 (50) by 2.   (Think:) What times 2 is
close to, but not more
than 50? 2 × 20 = 40

Put the 2 tens in the quotient.
Multiply the divisor by the
quotient.
Subtract.   (Think:) You have 1 ten left over.

Step 3 Bring down, divide the ones, and write in the amount.
Then, subtract.

$$\begin{array}{r} 2\,6 \\ 2\overline{)5\,3} \\ -4 \\ \hline 1\,3 \\ -1\,2 \\ \hline 1 \end{array}$$

Divide the 13 by 2.   (Think:) What times 2 is close
to, but not more than 13?
2 × 6 = 12

Put the 6 ones in the quotient.
Multiply the divisor by the quotient.
Subtract.   (Think:) You have 1 one left over.

53 ÷ 2 = 26 R 1

Divide. Use estimation to check.

1. 41 ÷ 2 _____

2. 67 ÷ 3 _____

3. 54 ÷ 4 _____

4. 89 ÷ 5 _____

Name _____ Date _____

Skills Practice

Two-Digit Quotients

Divide. Use estimation to check.

1. $3\overline{)272}$ _____

2. $4\overline{)230}$ _____

3. $5\overline{)351}$ _____

4. $9\overline{)180}$ _____

5. $3\overline{)150}$ _____

6. $7\overline{)496}$ _____

7. $9\overline{)685}$ _____

8. $6\overline{)283}$ _____

9. $5\overline{)454}$ _____

10. $8\overline{)260}$ _____

11. $9\overline{)643}$ _____

12. $3\overline{)103}$ _____

13. $6\overline{)457}$ _____

14. $7\overline{)143}$ _____

15. $4\overline{)165}$ _____

16. $642 \div 7$ _____

17. $250 \div 4$ _____

18. $435 \div 8$ _____

19. $187 \div 5$ _____

20. $567 \div 8$ _____

21. Janice and her 3 sisters earned $364 this summer doing yard work for a neighbor. They plan on splitting the money equally. How much will each girl get?

_____

22. A school was given 50 athletic balls to be split evenly between its sports teams. If there are 5 sports teams, how many balls will each team get?

_____

8–6

Reteach

Problem-Solving Investigation: Choose a Strategy

Choose the best strategy.

Using each of the SIX PROBLEM-SOLVING STRATEGIES:

- Use a four-step plan
- Work backward
- Make a table
- Look for a pattern
- Guess and check
- Act it out

1. A four-step plan - The four steps are understand, plan, solve, and check.

If you are given several facts, list what you already know and what you need to find out. To find this out, <u>think</u> about what you have to do mathematically.

Practice

Jill wants to buy jeans that cost $50, a shirt that costs $20, and a belt that costs $10. She has $100. Does she have enough money?

_____

2. Work backward

If you are given facts about the <u>present</u> and asked for information about the <u>past</u>, you need to work backward. Again, you'll have to <u>think</u> about what you have to do mathematically.

Practice

Jill bought the jeans for $40 and a shirt on sale for $5. She has $55 left. How much money did she start with? _____

3. Make a table

If you are given a list of things and there are different numbers for each thing, make a chart. Use the categories that you are given to make the rows and columns on your chart.
Think about what you have to do mathematically to the numbers in the chart.

Practice

Jill bought jeans for $40 and a belt for $5. Carol bought jeans for $10 and 3 belts for $5 each. Who spent more money?

Name _____ Date _____

Reteach

Problem Solving Investigation (continued)

4. A pattern

If you are given a row or list of numbers, colors, or objects, look for what repeats. Ask yourself what was done to the first thing in the list that was also done to the second and so on.

Practice

What is the next number in the pattern of 3, 12, 48, 192, _____?

5. Guess and check

Make a guess, then check to see if your guess is the solution to the problem. Keep guessing and checking until you find the solution.

Practice

What is the next number in the pattern of 5, 16, 49, 148, _____?

6. Act it out

If you are given information, and it would help to see what you are being told; act it out.

Practice

Fred has 3 bills that total $40. What bills does he have?

_____

8–6

Skills Practice

Problem-Solving Investigation: Choose a Strategy

Use any strategy to solve.

- Look for a pattern   • Make a table   • Work backward
- Act it out   • Guess and check

1. Russ bought 8 tubes of different color paint. Then, he traded 3 of his tubes for 10 of his friend's smaller tubes. How many does he have now?

   _____

2. Russ spent 45 minutes walking to a museum. The museum is 1 mile away from his home. He walked the first half mile in twice the time that he walked the second half. How long did it take Russ to walk the second half mile?

   _____

3. What is the next number in the pattern 3, 12, 48, 192, _____ ? What is the pattern?

   _____

4. Rod bought the following items for the party: 3 cakes, 2 vegetable trays, 4 bowls of vegetable dip, and 3 boxes of crackers.

Cakes	-	$5
Vegetable Tray	-	$3
Vegetable Dip	-	$1
Crackers	-	$2

   How much did he spend? _____

5. Jerry has 10 bills that equal $140. What are the bills?

   _____

6. Each day, Alex, a Husky dog, eats 4 cups of dog food, 2 treats that he is given, and 1 treat that he steals from Lily, a small Bicheon. Each day, Lily eats 1 cup for every 4 that Alex eats and only 1 of the treats that she gets. How much does Lily eat in a week?

   _____

Name _____ Date _____

Reteach

Three-Digit Quotients

Find 2)532.

hundreds	tens	ones
5	3	2

Step 1 **Divide the hundreds and write the amount in the hundreds box. Then, subtract.**

```
  2
2)532
 -4
  1
```

Divide the 5 (500) by 2.

Put the 2 hundreds in the quotient. Multiply the divisor by the quotient. Subtract.

Think: What times 2 is close to, but not more than 500.
$2 \times 200 = 400$

Think: You have 1 hundred left over.

Step 2 **Bring down. Divide the tens and write in the amount. Then, subtract.**

```
 26
2)532
 -4
 13
-12
  1
```

Divide the 130 by 2.

Put the 6 tens in the quotient. Multiply the divisor by the quotient. Subtract.

Think: What times 2 is close to, but not more than 130.
$2 \times 60 = 120$

Think: You have 1 ten left over.

Step 3 **Bring down. Divide the ones and write in the amount. Then, subtract.**

```
  266
2)532
 -4
 13
-12
  12
 -12
```

Divide the 12 by 2.

Put the 6 ones in the quotient. Multiply the divisor by the quotient. Subtract.

Think: What times 2 is close to, but not more than 12.
$2 \times 6 = 12$

Think: You have no remainder.

2)532 = 266

Divide. Use estimation to check.

1. 2)856 _____

2. 3)562 _____

3. 5)767 _____

4. 6)821 _____

Skills Practice

Three-Digit Quotients

Divide. Use estimation to check.

1. $6\overline{)689}$ _____

2. $4\overline{)470}$ _____

3. $9\overline{)999}$ _____

4. $5\overline{)942}$ _____

5. $3\overline{)545}$ _____

6. $7\overline{)868}$ _____

7. $5\overline{)681}$ _____

8. $3\overline{)498}$ _____

9. $2\overline{)642}$ _____

10. $4\overline{)868}$ _____

11. $3\overline{)765}$ _____

12. $8\overline{)912}$ _____

13. $3\overline{)946}$ _____

14. $4\overline{)523}$ _____

15. $868 \div 5$ _____

16. $874 \div 7$ _____

17. $672 \div 6$ _____

18. $347 \div 3$ _____

19. $591 \div 4$ _____

20. $671 \div 3$ _____

21. Ben and his 3 friends are planning to make box cars. They have collected 368 pieces of scraps from the junk yard. If they divide the pieces, how many will each boy get?

_____

22. Over the last 6 days, the boys have worked for 930 minutes trying to assemble their junk pieces. They worked for the same amount of time each day, from the time school got out to dark. How many minutes did they work each day?

_____

Name _____ Date _____

Reteach

Quotients with Zeros

Find 3)629. Follow the steps below.

Step 1. Divide the hundreds.	Step 2. Divide the tens.	Step 3. Divide the ones.
Think: $3 \times 2 = 600$ The first digit is in the hundreds place.	Bring down the tens. There are not enough tens to divide. Trade 2 tens for 20 ones.	Bring down the ones. Divide the ones.
$\begin{array}{r} 2 \\ 3)\overline{629} \\ -6 \\ \hline 0 \end{array}$ Multiply: $3 \times 2 = 6$ Subtract: $6 - 6 = 0$ Compare: $0 < 6$	$\begin{array}{r} 20 \\ 3)\overline{629} \\ -6 \\ \hline 02 \end{array}$ There are not enough tens to divide. Write a 0 in the quotient.	$\begin{array}{r} 209 \text{ R2} \\ 3)\overline{629} \\ -6 \\ \hline 029 \\ -27 \\ \hline 2 \end{array}$ Multiply: $3 \times 9 = 27$ Subtract: $29 - 27 = 2$

Check your answer: $209 \times 3 = 627$ $627 + 2 = 629$

Divide. Use estimation to check.

1.
$$3)\overline{9\ 2\ 6}$$
3 0 ☐ R ☐
−9

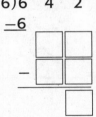

2.
$$6)\overline{6\ 4\ 2}$$
1 ☐ ☐
−6

3.
$$7)\overline{1\ 4\ 3}$$
☐ ☐ R ☐
−1 4

4. $4)\overline{\$816}$

5. $3)\overline{316}$

6. $2)\overline{615}$

7. $3)\overline{628}$

8. $4)\overline{438}$

9. $7)\overline{765}$

10. $2)\overline{361}$

11. $3)\overline{\$210}$

12. $912 \div 9 =$ _____

13. $662 \div 3 =$ _____

14. $905 \div 3 =$ _____

15. $452 \div 9 =$ _____

16. $965 \div 6 =$ _____

17. $734 \div 7 =$ _____

Name _____ Date _____

Skills Practice

Quotients with Zeros

Divide. Use estimation to check.

1. $3\overline{)620}$

2. $2\overline{)419}$

3. $9\overline{)92}$

4. $4\overline{)839}$

5. $6\overline{)\$630}$

6. $8\overline{)\$856}$

7. $7\overline{)\$763}$

8. $9\overline{)918}$

9. $5\overline{)549}$

10. $7\overline{)748}$

11. $8\overline{)812}$

12. $2\overline{)819}$

13. $6\overline{)620}$

14. $9\overline{)98}$

15. $3\overline{)211}$

16. $4\overline{)827}$

17. $5\overline{)544}$

18. $8\overline{)855}$

19. $6\overline{)657}$

20. $3\overline{)917}$

21. $2\overline{)819}$

22. $4\overline{)835}$

23. $7\overline{)727}$

24. $8\overline{)406}$

25. $823 \div 4 =$ _____

26. $704 \div 5 =$ _____

27. $981 \div 2 =$ _____

28. $920 \div 3 =$ _____

29. $916 \div 7 =$ _____

30. $845 \div 6 =$ _____

31. $885 \div 8 =$ _____

32. $954 \div 5 =$ _____

33. $965 \div 6 =$ _____

Solve.

34. Jenna earns \$636 in 6 months by babysitting. If divided evenly, how much is that a month? _____

35. A family of 4 spends \$824 when vacationing. If divided evenly, how much is that per person? _____

Name _____ Date _____

Reteach

Divide Greater Numbers

When you divide greater numbers, begin by deciding where to place the first digit in the quotient.

Divide 3,154 ÷ 6.

Think: You cannot divide 3 by 6. Divide 31 by 6. Write 5 in the quotient above the 1.

You can see the quotient will have 3 digits.

$$6\overline{)3{,}154} \quad \begin{array}{c} 5\_\_ \end{array}$$

Divide. Use estimation to check.

1. R☐
$$3\overline{)1{,}549}$$
$$-15$$

2. R☐
$$4\overline{)7{,}653}$$
$$-4$$

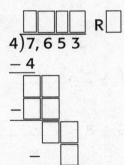

3. R☐
$$2\overline{)9{,}563}$$

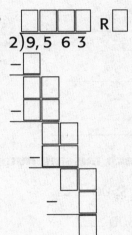

4. $5\overline{)3{,}472}$

5. $4\overline{)\$2{,}624}$

6. $8\overline{)9{,}275}$

7. $2\overline{)5{,}117}$

8. $7\overline{)4{,}986}$

9. $3\overline{)1{,}373}$

10. $6\overline{)4{,}738}$

11. $9\overline{)9{,}818}$

12. 1,671 ÷ 8 = _____

13. 3,393 ÷ 4 = _____

14. 7,087 ÷ 5 = _____

15. $9,217 ÷ 3 = _____

Name _____ Date _____

Skills Practice

Divide Greater Numbers

Divide. Use estimation to check.

1. $5\overline{)5,840}$　　　　2. $4\overline{)6,832}$　　　　3. $2\overline{)3,988}$

4. $6\overline{)\$9,384}$　　　　5. $8\overline{)3,767}$　　　　6. $7\overline{)4,513}$

7. $3\overline{)6,083}$　　　　8. $9\overline{)2,750}$　　　　9. $2\overline{)4,147}$

10. $6\overline{)3,199}$　　　　11. $5\overline{)3,079}$　　　　12. $7\overline{)6,213}$

13. $\$1,328 \div 4$ _____　　　　14. $7,895 \div 9$ _____

15. $5,620 \div 5 =$ _____　　　　16. $1,841 \div 2 =$ _____

17. $1,697 \div 6 =$ _____　　　　18. $7,986 \div 8 =$ _____

ALGEBRA Find each missing number.

19. $\$5,500 \div n = \$500$ ____

20. $7,200 \div v = 800$ ____

21. $4,000 \div r = 1,000$ ____

Solve.

22. The King School holds Junior Olympic games in its sports stadium for 3 days. Each day, every seat in the stadium is full. A total of 9,747 people come to the games. How many seats does the stadium have?

_____

23. The King School raises $5,286 by selling Junior Olympic banners. Each banner costs $6. How many banners does the school sell?

_____

Name _____ Date _____

Reteach

Three-Dimensional Figures

Three-dimensional figures are solids. This means they are not flat. For example, a square is flat, but a cube is a three-dimensional figure.

To describe the shape of a three-dimensional figure, you use:

- **face**: a flat side
- **edge**: where 2 **faces** meet
- **vertex**: where 3 or more faces meet, like a corner

To describe this three-dimensional figure, you would say it is a cube. It has:

- 6 faces
- 12 edges
- 8 vertices

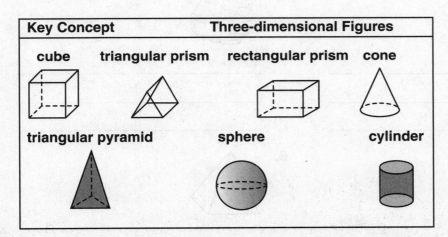

Key Concept — Three-dimensional Figures

cube   triangular prism   rectangular prism   cone

triangular pyramid   sphere   cylinder

Tell the number of faces, edges, and vertices. Then identify each figure.

1. _____

_____

_____

2.  _____

Identify the three-dimensional figure each net makes.

3. _____

4.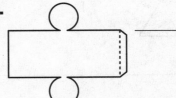

Name _____ Date _____

Skills Practice

Three-Dimensional Figures

Tell the number of faces, edges, and vertices. Then identify each figure.

1.

_____

_____

_____

2.

_____

_____

_____

3.

_____

_____

_____

4.

_____

_____

_____

5.

_____

_____

_____

6.

_____

_____

_____

Identify the three-dimensional figure each net makes.

7.

_____

8.

_____

9–2

Reteach

Two-Dimensional Figures

A polygon is a closed two-dimensional figure that has straight sides.
These figures are not polygons.

Open Figures	Closed Figures
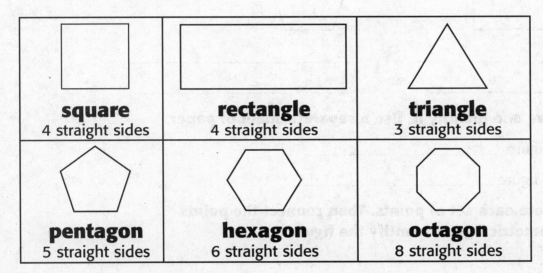	

These figures are polygons.

square 4 straight sides	**rectangle** 4 straight sides	**triangle** 3 straight sides
pentagon 5 straight sides	**hexagon** 6 straight sides	**octagon** 8 straight sides

Identify each polygon.

1.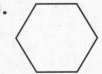

_____

2.

_____

3.

_____

4.

_____

5.

_____

6.

_____

Name _____ Date _____

Skills Practice

Two-Dimensional Figures

Tell whether each figure is *open* or *closed*. Is it a polygon? If so, classify the figure.

1.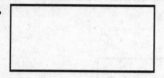

_____

_____

2.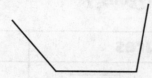

_____

_____

3.

_____

_____

4.

_____

_____

Draw the figure and identify it. Use a separate sheet of paper.

5. a 6-sided figure _____

6. an 8-sided figure _____

ALGEBRA Locate each set of points. Then connect the points to make a geometric figure. Identify the figure.

7. (2, 2), (4, 3), (3, 5)

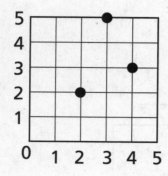

_____

8. (2, 2), (5, 2), (5, 3), (2, 3)

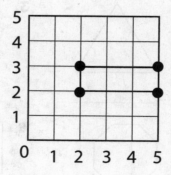

_____

Name _____ Date _____

Reteach

Problem-Solving Strategy: Look for a Pattern

What figures do you see in a repeated pattern?
How are the figures moved?

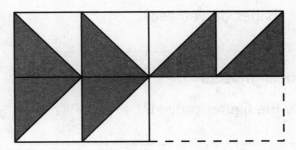

Step 1 Understand

Be sure you understand the problem.
Read carefully.

What do you know?

- The illustration shown is a tessellation.

What do you need to find?

- You need to identify

_____

_____

_____

Step 2 Plan

Make a plan.

Looking for a pattern will help you solve the problem.

Find shapes that look familiar. Look for a pattern to see how these shapes have been moved.

Name _____ Date _____

Reteach

Problem-Solving Strategy   (continued)

Step 3 Solve

Carry out your plan.

Look for shapes you know. What shapes do you see?

_____

To find how these shapes have been moved.

What is one way to describe how the figures moved?

_____

Step 4 Check

Is the solution reasonable?
Reread the problem.

Did you answer the question? Yes _____ No _____

What other strategies could you use to solve the problem?

_____

_____

Practice
Use data from this tessellation to solve.

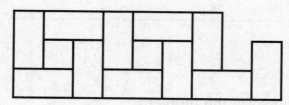

1. What shapes do you see in a repeated pattern? How are
   they moved?

_____

_____

Skills Practice

Problem-Solving Strategy: Look for a Pattern

Use data from this tessellation to solve problems 1–3.

1. What shapes do you see in a repeated pattern?

_____

2. How are the shapes moved?

_____

3. Suppose you extend this design. You have a total of 20 small right triangles. How many rhombi will there be in all?

_____

Solve. Use any strategy.

4. Aaron buys 5 Picasso T-shirts for his family. A large T-shirt costs $15 and a small T-shirt costs $12. Aaron spends $69. How many large T-shirts does he buy? How many small T-shirts does he buy?

_____

Strategy: _____

5. On May 15, 1990, a painting by Van Gogh sold for $75,000,000. Two days later, a painting by Renoir sold for $4,000,000 less than that amount. How much did Renoir's painting sell for?

_____

Strategy: _____

Skills Practice

Problem-Solving Strategy: Look for a Pattern

Use data from this tessellation to solve problems 1–3.

1. What shape do you see in a repeated pattern?

_____

2. How are the shapes moved?

_____

3. Suppose you extend this design. You have a total of 20 small light triangles. How many rhombuses will there be in all?

_____

Solve. Use any strategy.

4. Aaron buys 5 Packers T-shirts for his family. A large T-shirt costs $17, and a small T-shirt costs $12. Aaron spends $69. How many large T-shirts does he buy? How many small T-shirts does he buy?

Strategy _____

5. On April 26, 1990, a painting by Vincent van Gogh sold for $82,500,000. Two days later, a painting by Renoir sold for $4,000,000 less than that amount. How much did the Renoir painting sell for?

Strategy _____

Name _____ Date _____

Reteach

Angles

Angles are formed by two rays that have the same endpoint.

      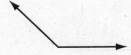

- A **right** angle forms a square corner.
- It measures 90°.
- It is formed by perpendicular lines.

- An **acute** angle is smaller than a right angle.
- It measures greater than 0° and less than 90°.

- An **obtuse** angle is bigger than a right angle.
- It measures greater than 90°, but less than 180°.

Identify each angle.

Classify each angle as *right*, *acute*, or *obtuse*. Use the corner of this paper to help you.

1.

2.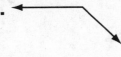

3.

4.

_____

_____

_____

_____

5.

6.

7.

8.

_____

_____

_____

_____

Complete.

9.

This triangle has

3 _____ angles.

10.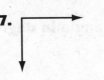

This kite has

2 _____ angles and

2 _____ angles.

11.

This pentagon has

2 _____ angles,

2 _____ angles

and 1 _____ angle.

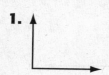

Name _____   Date _____

Skills Practice

Angles

Classify each angle as *right, acute,* or *obtuse*.

1. _____   2. _____   3. _____

4. _____   5. _____   6. _____

Write the measure of the angle in degrees and as a fraction of a full turn.

7. _____   8. _____   9. _____

Write the measure of the angle in degrees and classify each angle as *right, acute,* or *obtuse*.

10.

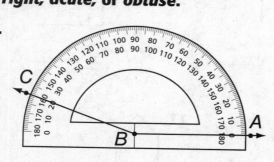

_____

11.

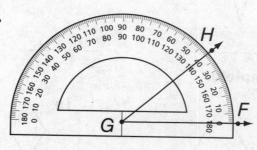

_____

Name _____ Date _____

Reteach

Triangles

You can classify a triangle by the lengths of its sides or the measures of its angles.

An **isosceles triangle** has at least two sides of equal length.

An **equilateral triangle** has three sides of equal length.

A **scalene triangle** has no sides of equal length.

An **acute triangle** has three acute angles (less than 90°).

A **right triangle** has one right angle (exactly 90°).

An **obtuse triangle** has one obtuse angle (greater than 90° and less than 180°).

Classify each triangle. Use *acute*, *right*, or *obtuse* and *isosceles*, *equilateral*, or *scalene*.

1.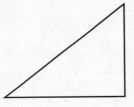

_____

_____

2.

_____

_____

3.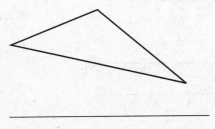

_____

_____

4.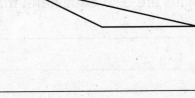

_____

_____

Name _____ Date _____

Skills Practice

Triangles

**Classify each triangle. Use *acute*, *right*, or *obtuse* and
equilateral, *isosceles*, or *scalene*.**

1.

_____

_____

2.

_____

_____

Define each term.

3. scalene

_____

4. obtuse

_____

5. equilateral

_____

Tell if each statement is *true* or *false*. Explain why.

6. Equilateral triangles are triangles where all three sides have
   different lengths.

_____

_____

7. Some right triangles are also equilateral triangles.

_____

_____

Solve.

8. Sue's half sandwich is 5 inches on one side, 3 inches on another,
   and 4 inches on the third side. What kind of triangle is it?

_____

9-6

Reteach

Quadrilaterals

All quadrilaterals have 4 sides and 4 angles.

A **square** has 4 equal sides and 4 right angles.

A **rhombus** has 4 equal sides. Its opposite sides are parallel.

A **rectangle** has 4 right angles. Its opposite sides are equal and parallel.

A **trapezoid** has 1 pair of parallel sides.

A **parallelogram** has opposite sides that are equal and parallel.

Classify each quadrilateral in as many ways as you can.

1. _____

2. _____

3. _____

4. This quadrilateral has opposite sides that are equal and parallel.
   What quadrilateral is it? _____

5. True or false.
   A rectangle is a parallelogram. _____

6. How are a rhombus and a trapezoid similar?

   _____

   _____

   _____

Name _____ Date _____

Skills Practice

Quadrilaterals

Write the type of quadrilateral that best describes the shape.

1.

2.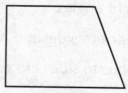

3.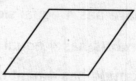

_____   _____   _____

Tell if each statement is *true* or *false*. Explain why.

4. All rectangles are parallelograms. _____

_____

5. All squares are rhombuses. _____

_____

6. Some right triangles are also equilateral triangles. _____

_____

Solve.

7. Sue's desk has equal sides of 20 inches and 4 right angles.
   Nancy's desk has two sides of 20 inches, two sides of 30 inches,
   and 4 right angles. Both say their desks are rectangles.
   Who is correct?

_____

8. Mike makes a square out of wooden sticks. He pushes
   one corner of the square and makes a rhombus. How are
   the square and rhombus alike? How are they different?

_____

_____

_____

_____

172

Name _____ Date _____

Reteach

Problem-Solving Investigation: Choose a Strategy

There are many ways to solve most math problems. You will decide which method works best for you when you read the problems.

Maria is trying to put her brother's blocks the way they were when she found them. They were in a neat rectangle. Use the polygons below to form a rectangle:

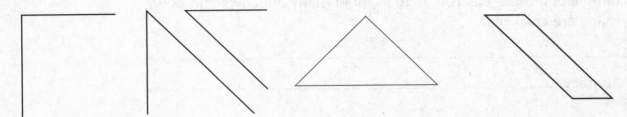

Understand	You know that you need to use the five polygons to form a rectangle. You need to find out how to arrange the polygons to form a rectangle.
Plan	Choose a strategy. This problem has pieces that need to be moved around to fit in a certain way. You could draw these pieces on paper, cut them out, and move them around to see how they fit. Use the act it out strategy to solve the problem.
Solve	Arrange the polygons in different ways until you form a rectangle:
Check	Look back at the problem. Check to see if you are correct: The shape you formed has 4 right angles, with opposite sides parallel. The sides are not all the same size. You made a rectangle.

Name _____ Date _____

Reteach

Problem-Solving Investigation (continued)

Use any method shown below to solve. Tell what method you used.

- Act it out
- Guess and check
- Make a table

1. A farmer has cows and chickens. Juan counted 296 legs in the farmyard. If there are 100 animals, how many are cows and how many are chickens?

_____

Strategy: _____

2. Melissa has $20. She earns $9 a week babysitting. Will she be able to buy a bike that costs $150 in 15 weeks?

_____

Strategy: _____

3. Drew bought his lunch for $6. Then he paid $8 for admission to the skate park. Then he paid $3 to ride the bus home. Now he has $2. How much money did Drew start with?

_____

Strategy: _____

4. Abby paid for lunch with $15. She got back $4. If her salad cost $3, and her water cost $2, how much was the turkey sandwich?

_____

Strategy: _____

5. Colin sold muffins for the school's bake sale. He sold each muffin for $1.50. If he earned $48, how many muffins did he sell?

_____

Strategy: _____

Name _____ Date _____

Skills Practice

Problem-Solving Investigation: Choose a Strategy

Use any method shown below to solve. Tell what method you used.

- Act it out
- Guess and check

- Make a table
- Look for a pattern

1. A group of kids were riding bikes. Jessica counted 38 wheels. If there are 15 kids, how many are riding bikes with training wheels and how many are riding bikes without training wheels?

_____

Strategy: _____

2. Nicholas practices lacrosse for 75 minutes a day during the week and 90 minutes a day on weekends. Does he practice lacrosse for 15 hours each week?

_____

Strategy: _____

3. Kayla sat down to begin her homework at 4:15. After school, her bus ride home is 15 minutes. Then she had a snack and talked with her friends for 25 minutes. She also did her chores for 20 minutes before beginning her homework. What time does

Kayla's school end? _____

Strategy: _____

4. What are the next three animals in the pattern if this pattern continues?

_____

Strategy: _____

5. Tyler is bringing napkins for his grade's picnic. There are 92 people coming to the picnic. He found napkins in packages of 12. How many packages does Tyler need to bring? _____

Strategy: _____

Name ______________________ Date ______________

10–1 Reteach

Locate Points on a Number Line

A number line is a line that represents numbers as points.

Write the number represented by each letter.

To find out what number is represented by each letter we need to determine the scale of the number line and use the numbers provided to count and find out what each letter is.

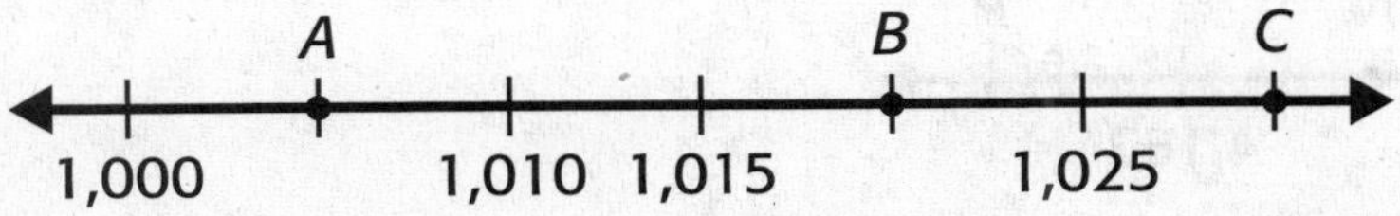
A
B
C
1,000
1,010
1,015
1,025

Look at the number line above. We can see that the scale for the number line is in five unit intervals. If we fill in the missing numbers on the number line, we can determine the numbers represented by *A*, *B*, and *C*.

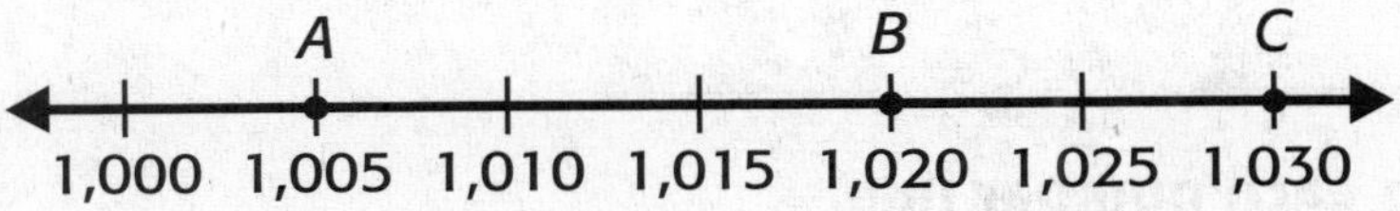
A
B
C
1,000
1,005
1,010
1,015
1,020
1,025
1,030

A = 1,005 *B* = 1,020 *C* = 1,030

Write the number represented by each letter.

1.

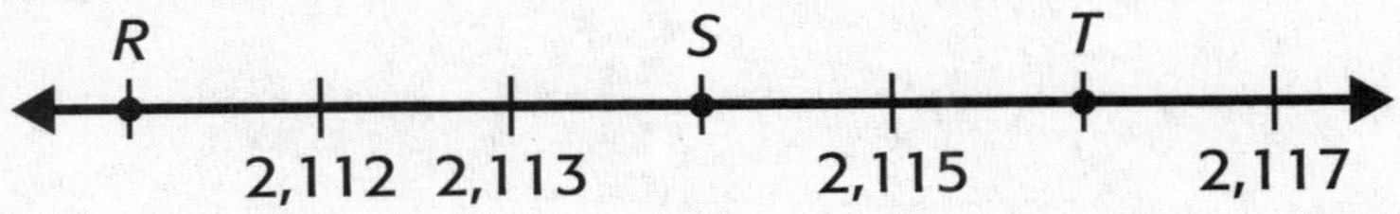
R
S
T
2,112
2,113
2,115
2,117

R = __________ *S* = __________ *T* = __________

2.

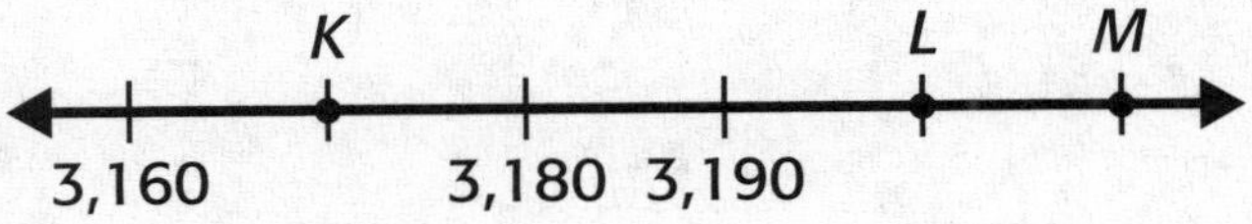
K
L
M
3,160
3,180
3,190

K = __________ *L* = __________ *M* = __________

Write the number *W* represents on each number line.

3.

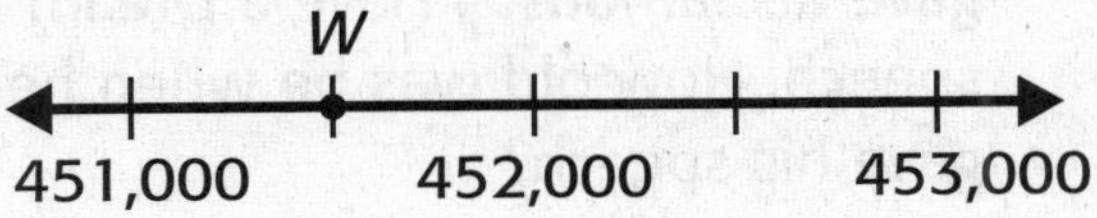
W
451,000
452,000
453,000

W = __________

4.

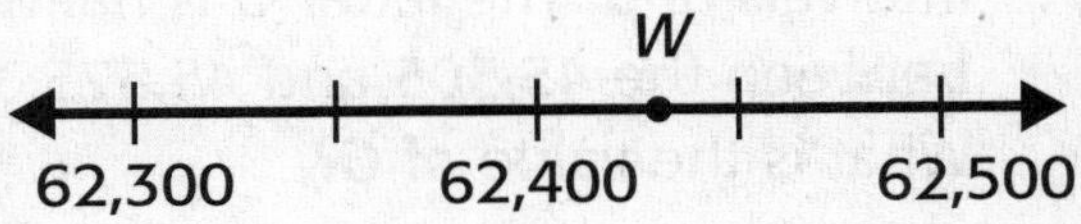
W
62,300
62,400
62,500

W = __________

Name _____ Date _____

Skills Practice

Locate Points on a Number Line

Write the number represented by each letter.

1.

X = _____ W = _____ Z = _____

2.

M = _____ N = _____ P = _____

3.

A = _____ B = _____ C = _____

Write the number D represents on each number line.

4.

D = _____

5.

D = _____

Solve.

6. A number line starts with 45,505 and ends with 45,525. It is marked with intervals of 5. The letter G is halfway between the 45,505 and 45,525. What is the value of G?

_____

7. A timeline shows that in 1929 Martin Luther King Jr. was born. In 1963 he gave his famous "I Have a Dream" speech. How old was he when he gave his speech?

_____

10-2

Reteach

Lines, Line Segments, and Rays

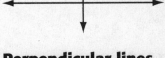 A **line** goes on forever in both directions	A **line segment** is part of a line. It has two endpoints.	A **ray** has one endpoint.
Parallel lines never meet.	**Intersecting lines** meet.	**Perpendicular lines** form square corners.

Identify each figure.

1.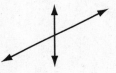

_____

2.

_____

3.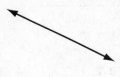

_____

4.

_____

5.

_____

6.

_____

7.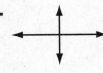

_____

_____

8.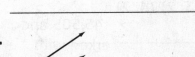

_____

_____

Name _____ Date _____

Skills Practice

Lines, Line Segments, and Rays

Describe the figure.

1.
A ———— B

_____

2. I   L
K   J

_____

_____

_____

3. C
    D →

_____

4. *l* →
    ←

_____

5. Q
S ——+—— T
    R

_____

_____

_____

6. M   N →
    ●   ●

    O   P →
    ●   ●

_____

_____

_____

ALGEBRA Locate each set of points. Then connect the points to draw line segments. Classify them as perpendicular or parallel.

7. Line segment *OP*:
    (1, 4) (2, 4) (3, 4) (4, 4)

    Line segment *QR*:
    (1, 2) (2, 2) (3, 2) (4, 2)

_____

6 ● ● ● ● ● ●
5 ● ● ● ● ● ●
4 ● ● ● ● ● ●
3 ● ● ● ● ● ●
2 ● ● ● ● ● ●
1 ● ● ● ● ● ●
  1 2 3 4 5 6

Name _____ Date _____

Reteach

Problem-Solving Strategy: Make an Organized List

Otto plays a game. He spins the two spinners shown below and finds the product of the numbers he lands on. What products can Otto make?

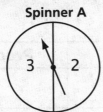

Spinner A

Spinner B

Step 1 Understand	**Be sure you understand the problem.** Read carefully. What facts do you know? • Spinner A is marked _____ and Spinner B is marked _____ What do you need to find? • What _____ Otto can make.
Step 2 Plan	**Make a plan.** **Choose a strategy.** You can make an organized list to solve the problem. **Remember:** A product is the answer to a multiplication problem.

Name _____ Date _____

Reteach

Problem-Solving Strategy *(continued)*

Step 3 **Solve**	**Carry out your plan.** Make a list of all the possible spinner products. Then find each product.

Spinner A		Spinner B		Product
	×		=	
	×		=	
	×		=	
	×		=	
	×		=	
	×		=	

What products can Otto make? _____

Step 4 **Check**	**Is the solution reasonable?** Reread the problem. Have you answered the question? _____ How can you check your answer? _____ _____ _____ _____ _____

Practice

1. A spinner has 3 equal sections that are white, yellow, and green. Another spinner has 3 equal sections that are blue, purple, and red. How many different combinations of colors are possible if you spin each spinner once? _____

10-3

Skills Practice

Problem-Solving Strategy: Make an Organized List

Solve. Use the make an organized list strategy.

1. Juanita had 12 pencils in a box. She needed 144 for a school wide test. How many boxes will she need?

   _____

2. Jared runs 4 laps around the track 3 times a week. How many laps does he run in 1 month? 6 weeks?

   _____

   _____

3. Alicia bought 2 sweaters and one pair of jeans. The jeans cost twice the amount of the sweaters. She gave the cashier 4 twenty-dollar bills, and she received $5 back in change. How much did the sweaters cost? How much were the jeans?

   _____

   _____

4. Ally has a choice of 3 different pairs of socks including red, white, or black. If she reaches into her drawer and randomly chooses a pair, what is the probability that she will choose white?

   _____

5. Drake wants to buy a CD for his mother's birthday. It costs $18. He makes $4 for mowing the lawn, and $5 for cleaning. How many times must he do each chore to make enough money for the CD?

   _____

   _____

6. Juan could make banana bread, apple bread, or muffins. He could use whole wheat flour or white flour. How many possible combinations can he make?

   _____

Skills Practice

Problem-Solving Strategy: Make an Organized List

Solve. Use this, make an organized list strategy.

1. Jamie had 12 pencils in a box. She added 1/2 for a stack of the test. How many boxes will she need?

2. Jared runs 4 laps around the track 3 times a week. How many laps does he run in 1 month, 4 weeks?

3. Alicia bought 7 candies and one pair of earrings for a dollar coat with the amount of the issues — what's the past the cashier seven-dollar bills and 5 quarters and 50 pennies change. How much change was left? How much were the penny?

4. Ally has a choice of 3 different caps, checks, plaid, or white, or blank shirts: red, blue, purple, and white, pink, or purple clothes. What is the probability that she will choose white.

5. Drake wants to buy a CD for his mother's birthday. It costs $16. He makes $4 for mowing the lawn and $3 for raking. How many times must he do each chore to make enough money for the CD?

6. Juan could make bread, apple bread, or muffin. He could use whole wheat flour or white flour. How many combinations can he make?

Name _____ Date _____

Reteach

Find Points on a Grid

The grid shows the location of rides at an amusement park.

Where is the Space Ride located? Start at 0. Go right 1, and then go up 2. You can write the location of the Space Ride as the ordered pair (1, 2).

In an ordered pair, the first number tells you how far to go to the right. The second number tells you how far to go up.

Try this. Go right 5, and then go up 1.

(5, 1) ⟵ ordered pair

Which ride do you find?

_____

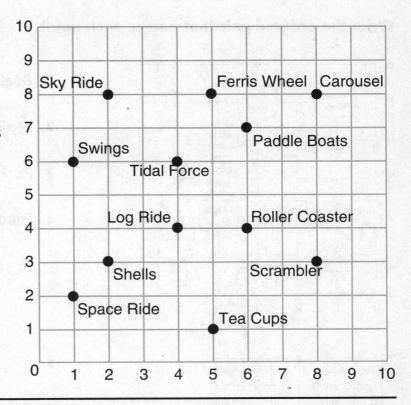

Complete. Use the grid above.

1. Start at 0. Go right 8, and then go up 3.

   The ordered pair is (8, __).

   What is here? _____

2. Start at 0. Go right 2, and then go up 8.

   The ordered pair is _____.

   What is here? _____

3. Start at 0. Go right 4, and then go up 4.

   The ordered pair is (__, 4).

   What is here? _____

4. Start at 0. Go right 6, and then go up 7.

   The ordered pair is _____.

   What is here? _____

Identify the ride that is located at each ordered pair.

5. (5, 8) _____

6. (1, 6) _____

7. (2, 3) _____

8. (6, 4) _____

9. (4, 6) _____

10. (8, 8) _____

Name _____ Date _____

Skills Practice

Find Points on a Grid

Write the ordered pair that names each point.

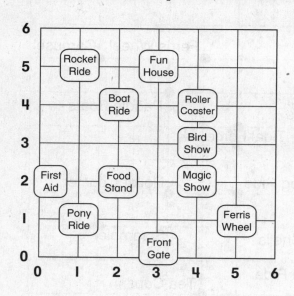

1. Boat Ride _____

2. Ferris Wheel _____

3. Rocket Ride _____

4. Food Stand _____

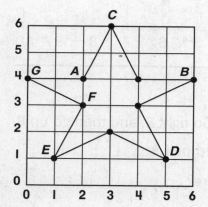

5. B _____

6. D _____

7. E _____

8. F _____

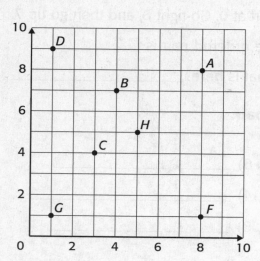

9. A _____

10. D _____

11. F _____

12. G _____

Name _____ Date _____

Reteach

Rotations, Reflections, and Translations

A geometric figure goes through a transformation when it changes location.

Using this geometric figure, we can transform it three ways.

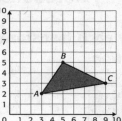

Rotation (Turn)	Reflection (Flip)	Translation (Slide)
A rotation is a transformation in which a figure is rotated or turned around a point. Rotate the figure 180 degrees counter-clockwise from point *B*.	A reflection is a transformation that flips a figure across a line to make a mirror image of that figure. Reflect the figure across the line $y = 6$.	A translation is transformation that moves a figure in a vertical, horizontal or diagonal direction. Translate the figure 4 up and 2 left.
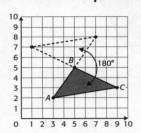	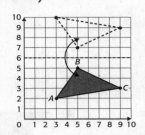	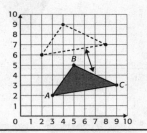

Draw the transformation.

1.

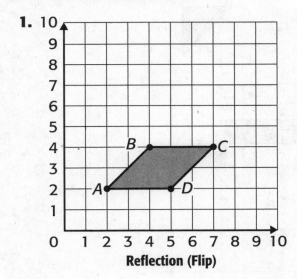

Reflection (Flip)

2.

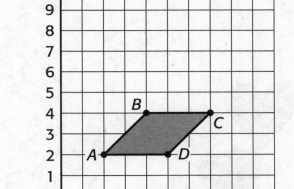

Rotation (Turn)

187

10-5

Skills Practice

Rotations, Reflections, and Translations

Identify each transformation. Write *rotation*, *reflection*, or *translation*.

1.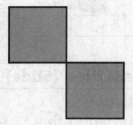

_____

2.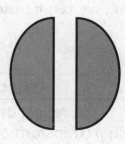

_____

3.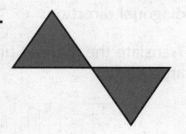

_____

4.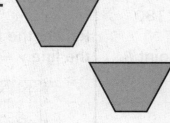

_____

5.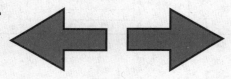

_____

6.

_____

7.

_____

8.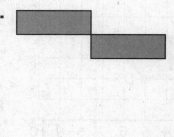

_____

10-6

Reteach

Problem-Solving Investigation: Choose a Strategy

Joel went to a pumpkin patch. He saw 10 pumpkins in each row. There were 8 rows on one side of the road, and 9 rows on the other. How many pumpkins were there?

Step 1 Understand	**Be sure you understand the problem.** What facts do you know? • Joel went to a pumpkin patch. • There were _____ pumpkins in each row. • There were _____ rows on one side of the road. • There were _____ rows on the other side of the road.
Step 2 Plan	**Make a plan.** Choose a strategy. You may draw a picture. Draw the road, rows, and pumpkins. You can also make a model.
Step 3 Solve	Carry out your plan. **Plan 1** Draw a picture. Draw the 10 pumpkins in each of the 8 rows on one side of the road and 9 rows on the other side. Add them up. $10+10+10+10+10+10+10+10 = 80$ $10+10+10+10+10+10+10+10+10 = 90$ $80 + 90 = 170$ pumpkins **Plan 2** Use counters to represent rows. Decide what facts you know. Plan what you will do and in what order. Use your plan to solve the problem. Then check your solution to make sure it makes sense.

Name _____ Date _____

Reteach (continued)

Problem-Solving Investigation

Step 4 Check	Is the solution reasonable? Reread the problem. How can you check your answer?

Solve using any strategy shown below.

- Use logical reasoning
- Make a model
- Draw a picture
- Work backward
- Make an organized list

1. Jen has 12 juice boxes in a case. She needs 96 boxes for a school picnic. How many cases will she need to bring? _____

2. Marsha rides her horse 3 times a week for 2 hours at a time. How many hours does she ride her horse in 2 weeks? 3 weeks?

   _____

3. Nicholas bought 4 hamburgers and 2 salads. He gave the cashier 2 ten-dollar bills. If he received $2 back, how much did he pay for the food? _____

4. Collin packed sandwiches for a field trip lunch. He had 12 turkey, 10 peanut butter, and 15 ham. Nine of the children brought their own sandwiches, so how many total children went on the field trip? _____

5. For your birthday, your parents bought you a bicycle for $89 and a new coat for $155. If they still have $69 left, how much money did they start out with? _____

6. Juanita made a science fair display with a spider web that spanned a 6-foot by 4-foot area. If she placed 10 spiders in each square foot, how many spiders were there? _____

7. Olivia is twice as old as three times the age of her younger brother, Ricardo. Ricardo is 4 years old. How old is Olivia?

   _____

10-6

Skills Practice

Problem-Solving Investigation: Choose a Strategy

Solve using any strategy shown below.

- Use logical reasoning
- Make a model
- Draw a picture
- Work backward
- Make an organized list

1. Roberto has 90 vitamins in a bottle. If he takes the vitamins twice

   a day, how many days will the bottle last? _____

2. Luis rides a motor scooter to work and home every day. He has to
   go 40 miles one way. How many miles will he put on the motor
   scooter in 7 days? 10 days?

   _____

   _____

3. Martin can choose from white socks, black socks, or colored socks,
   with leather shoes or tennis shoes. How many combinations of

   shoes and socks can he wear? _____

4. Your parents bought you a new video game system for $200
   and $90 worth of games. If they still have $40 left, how much

   money did they start out with? _____

5. Rafael wants to plant 8 bushes in his yard. Each bush needs a 2
   square foot area. How many square feet does he need in the yard

   for the bushes? _____

6. Kristen sold 60 rolls of wrapping paper. She sold 12 rolls of striped
   paper and 18 rolls of green paper. How many rolls were red?

   _____

Name _____ Date _____

Reteach

Congruent Figures

Similar Figures	**Congruent Figures**	**Not congruent Not similar**
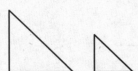		
• *same* shape • different sizes	• *same* shape • *same* size	• not the same shape • not the same size

To see if figures are congruent, trace one figure. If it fits exactly on top of the other figure, the two figures are congruent.

Tell whether the figures appear to be congruent. Write *yes* or *no*.

1.

_____

2.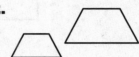

_____

3.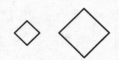

_____

4.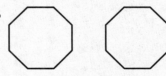

_____

5.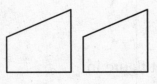

_____

6.

_____

Name _____ Date _____

Skills Practice

Congruent Figures

Tell whether the figures appear to be congruent. Write *yes* or *no*.

1. 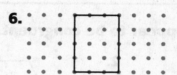 _____

2.  _____

3. _____

4. _____

**Copy each figure on a separate piece of dot paper.
Then draw one congruent figure.**

5.

6.

7.

8.

9.

10.

ALGEBRA Use separate grid paper.

11. Draw a figure on a coordinate grid. Then draw a congruent figure in another quadrant. Write the ordered pairs for all vertices.

10-8

Reteach

Symmetry

Follow these steps to find out if a figure has bilateral symmetry.

Trace Figure A and cut it out. Fold it along one of the dashed lines. The two halves match. The dashed line is a **line of symmetry**. The figure has **bilateral symmetry**. Unfold the figure. Fold the figure along the other dashed lines. The halves match, so all the lines are lines of symmetry.

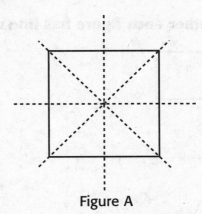

Figure A

Tell whether each figure has line symmetry. Write *yes* or *no*.

1.

_____

2.

_____

3.

_____

4.

_____

5.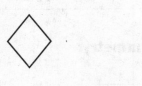

_____

6.

_____

Name _____ Date _____

Skills Practice
Symmetry

Tell whether each figure has line symmetry. Write *yes* or *no*.

1.

_____

2.

_____

3.

_____

4.

_____

Tell whether the dotted line is a line of symmetry. Write *yes* or *no*.

5.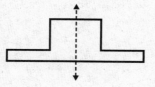

_____

6.

_____

7.

_____

8.

_____

9.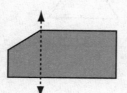

_____

10.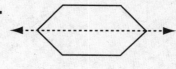

_____

11. On a separate sheet of paper, draw a figure with **bilateral symmetry**.

_____

Name _____ Date _____

Reteach

Customary Units of Length

Many different customary units measure length. Different tools are used to measure these units. For instance, you would probably not measure the distance between your house and the grocery store in inches with a ruler. You would probably measure it with the odometer in your parents' car. The odometer measures the length in miles.

What unit would you use to measure the length of your school's gym?

Step 1 Determine the general size of the gym.

The gym is very large, so larger units are probably the better choice. Should you use miles or yards?

Step 2 Using estimation, determine whether miles or yards is a more reasonable measurement for the gym.

The gym is much less than a mile long, so yards are the best choice. You would use a yardstick to measure the gym.

List an item that would be about the same length as each measurement given.

1. 5 inches _____

2. 10 feet _____

3. 5 miles _____

4. 1 inch _____

5. 2 yards _____

6. 30 feet _____

What customary unit would you use to measure the following?

7. insect _____

8. playground _____

9. distance from your house to Chicago _____

10. pencil _____

11. aquarium _____

12. soccer field _____

Skills Practice

Customary Units of Length

List two items that would be about the same length as each measurement given.

1. 1 inch _____

2. 13 yards _____

3. 4 inches _____

4. 1 foot _____

5. $\frac{1}{2}$ inch _____

6. 10 miles _____

What customary unit would you use to measure the following?

7. baseball _____

8. driveway _____

9. distance from New York to Los Angeles _____

10. train _____

11. telephone _____

12. refrigerator _____

Solve.

13. Jenny has 3 bananas that are 6 inches long. If she lays them

    end-to-end, how long will the line of bananas be? _____

14. Brice needs 2 feet of ribbon to tie a bow around a birthday
    present. He has 3 feet. Does he have enough?

    _____

15. What tool would you use to measure a football field? In what unit

    will your results be? _____

Name _____ Date _____

Reteach

Convert Customary Units of Length

Amy and her mother walk $\frac{1}{2}$ mile every Saturday morning to go to the public library. How many feet do they walk?

| **Step 1:** | Find the conversion rate between miles and feet. |
| | 1 mile = 5,280 ft |

Step 2:	Since Amy and her mother walk half a mile, divide the number of feet by two.
	1 mile = 5,280 ft
	$\frac{5,280}{2} = 2,640$
	Therefore, Amy and her mother walked 2,640 feet.

Convert 14 yards to feet.

1 yard = 3 feet

To perform the conversion, multiply 14 by 3.

14 yd = 42 ft

Complete.

1. 5 ft = _____ in.

2. 108 inches = _____ yd

3. 36 in. = _____ ft

4. _____ in. = 20 ft

5. 3 mi = _____ yd

6. 5 ft 5 in. = _____ in.

Name _____ Date _____

Skills Practice

Convert Customary Units of Length

Convert.

1. 90 ft = _____ in.

2. 6 yd = _____ ft

3. 23,760 ft = _____ mi

4. _____ in. = 11 ft

5. 2 mi = _____ yd

6. 5 ft 10 in. = _____ in.

7. 24 ft = _____ yd

8. 45 ft = _____ yd

9. _____ in. = 1 yd

10. _____ mi = 15,840 ft

11. 60 ft = _____ yd

12. 5 mi = _____ yd

13. _____ ft = 9 in.

14. 2 ft = _____ in.

15. 5,280 ft = _____ mi

16. 18 in = _____ yd

17. 5 yd = _____ in.

18. Kate walks half a mile home everyday after school. How many yards does she walk?

_____

19. The Millers' house is 25 yards away from Mrs. Shapiro's house. How many feet apart are the two houses?

_____

Name _____ Date _____

Reteach

Problem-Solving Strategy: Solve a Simpler Problem

Josh buys a 5-pound watermelon for $0.49 per pound and 2 pounds of grapes for $1.29 per pound. Sabrina buys an 8-pound watermelon for $0.29 per pound and 3 pounds of grapes for $0.99 per pound. Who spends more money? How much more?

Step 1. Understand	**Be sure you understand the problem.** Read carefully. What do you know?
	• Josh buys _____ pounds of watermelon for _____ per pound.
	  He also buys _____ pounds of grapes for _____ per pound.
	• Sabrina buys _____ pounds of watermelon for _____ per pound.
	  She also buys _____ pounds of grapes for _____ per pound.
	What do you need to find?
	• You need to find
	  _____

Step 2. Plan	**Make a plan.** Solve a simpler problem. Use simpler numbers to make up a problem similar to the one you need to solve. Then solve the real problem the same way.

Name _____ Date _____

Reteach

Problem-Solving Strategy (continued)

Step 3. **Solve**	**Carry out your plan.**
	 Create a simpler problem.
	
	 Josh: watermelon: $0.50 per lb grapes: $1.30 per lb
	
	 $5 \times \$0.50 = $ **$2.50** $2 \times \$1.30 = $ **$2.60**
	 $2.50 + **$2.60** = $5.10
	
	 Sabrina: watermelon: $0.30 per lb grapes: $1.00 per lb
	
	 $8 \times \$0.30 = $ **$2.40** $3 \times \$1.00 = $ **$3.00**
	 $2.40 + **$3.00** = $5.40
	
	 Solve the problem using the real numbers.
	 Josh: $5 \text{ lb} \times \$0.49 = $ **$2.45** $2 \text{ lb} \times \$1.29 = $ **$2.58**
	                              $2.45 + **$2.58** = $5.03
	
	 Sabrina: $8 \text{ lb} \times \$0.29 = \$2.32$ $3 \text{ lb} \times \$0.99 = $ **$2.97**
	                              $2.32 + **$2.97** = $5.29
	
	 $5.29 − $5.03 = $0.26 Sabrina spends $0.26 more.

Step 4. **Check**	**Is the solution reasonable?** Reread the problem. Does your answer make sense? Explain. _____ _____

Solve. Use the solve a simpler problem strategy.

1. Robert buys 4 pounds of apples for $0.89 per pound and 3 pounds of grapes for $1.09 per pound. Which fruit does he spend

   more on? How much more? _____

2. Kyle buys 7 pounds of cashew nuts, 5 pounds of walnuts, and 2 pounds of peanuts. Jane buys 3 pounds of cashew nuts, 4 pounds of walnuts, and 8 pounds of peanuts. Who buys more nuts? How much more?

Name _____ Date _____

Skills Practice

Problem-Solving Strategy: Solve a Simpler Problem

Solve. Use the solve a simpler problem strategy.

1. Sandwiches cost $5. Drinks cost $1. How much does it cost to buy 2 sandwiches and 3 drinks? _____

2. A customer pays $3.95 for 5 pounds of apples. What is the price for 1 pound of apples? _____

3. Recipe A uses $\frac{1}{2}$ cup of chicken broth and $\frac{1}{4}$ cup of water. Recipe B uses $\frac{1}{3}$ cup of chicken broth and $\frac{1}{3}$ cup of water. Which recipe uses more liquid? _____

4. Tracy buys $\frac{3}{4}$ pound of roast beef, $\frac{1}{2}$ pound of turkey, and $\frac{3}{8}$ pound of ham. Ken buys $\frac{1}{4}$ pound of roast beef, $\frac{1}{2}$ pound of turkey, and $\frac{3}{8}$ pound of ham. Who buys more meat? How much more does that person buy? _____

Solve. Use any strategy.

5. There are 24 plants in a garden. There are 4 more tomato plants than red pepper plants. There are twice as many red pepper plants as green pepper plants. How many of each kind of plant is in the garden?

   _____

   _____

   Strategy: _____

6. The Yogurt Cart has the following 3 flavors: chocolate, vanilla, and strawberry. Yogurt comes in a cup or a cone. You can have no sprinkles, chocolate sprinkles, or rainbow sprinkles. How many different choices are there? _____

   Strategy: _____

7. An ounce of cheddar cheese has 114 calories. An ounce of Brie cheese has 95 calories. How many more calories does an ounce of cheddar cheese have than an ounce of Brie cheese?

   _____

   Strategy: _____

Name _____ Date _____

Reteach

Metric Units of Length

Earlier in Chapter 11, you learned how to measure length using customary units. Now, you will learn how to measure length using metric units. The metric system measures length in millimeters, centimeters, meters, and kilometers.

What unit would you use to measure the length of your hand?

Step 1	Decide whether larger or smaller units would be best.
	Since a hand is fairly small, a smaller unit of measurement would probably be best.
Step 2	Using estimation, determine whether millimeters or centimeters is a more reasonable measurement for your hand.
	Though you *could* measure your hand in millimeters, centimeters is probably a more reasonable choice
	So, you would use centimeters to measure the length of your hand.

Choose the best estimate.

1. a leaf
   A. 20 millimeters   **C.** 20 meters
   B. 20 kilometers   **D.** 20 centimeters

   1. _____

2. an airport runway
   F. 1 kilometer   **H.** 1 meter
   G. 1 millimeter   **J.** 1 centimeter

   2. _____

3. a fingernail
   A. 6 meters   **C.** 6 millimeters
   B. 6 kilometers   **D.** 6 centimeters

   3. _____

4. a schoolbus
   F. 10 centimeters   **H.** 10 kilometers
   G. 10 meters   **J.** 10 millimeters

   4. _____

5. A car is about 2 meters long. Name something else that is two

   meters long. _____

Name _____ Date _____

Skills Practice

Metric Units of Length

Measure each object to the nearest centimeter.

1. 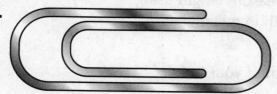 _____

2. _____

3. _____

4. _____

Choose the best estimate. Circle your estimate.

5. pencil

    A. 25 millimeters   **C.** 25 meters

    B. 25 centimeters   **D.** 25 kilometers

6. insect egg

    F. 2 millimeters   **H.** 2 meters

    G. 2 centimeters   **J.** 2 kilometers

7. giraffe

    A. 5 millimeters   **C.** 5 meters

    B. 5 centimeters   **D.** 5 kilometers

Name _____ Date _____

Reteach

Measure Perimeter

Perimeter is the distance around a closed figure. To find the perimeter, add the lengths of all the sides.

```
  10 ft
  15 ft
  10 ft
+ 15 ft
  50 ft
```

```
        15 ft
    ┌──────────┐
10 ft│          │10 ft
    └──────────┘
        15 ft
```

The perimeter of the rectangle is 50 feet.

Find the perimeter of each figure.

1.

4 in. 4 in.

4 in.

_____ + _____ + _____ = _____

2.

5 in.

5 in.   5 in.

5 in.

_____ + _____ + _____ + _____ = _____

3. 4 ft 4 ft 3 ft _____	**4.** 3 ft 3 ft 3 ft 3 ft _____	**5.** 4 in. 5 in. 3 in. 6 in. _____
6. 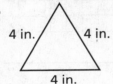 7 m 5 m 5 m 7 m _____	**7.** 6 dm 6 dm 6 dm 6 dm 6 dm 6 dm _____	**8.** 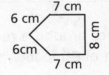 7 cm 6 cm 6cm 8 cm 7 cm _____

11-5

Skills Practice

Measure Perimeter

Find the perimeter of each figure.

1.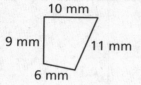

_____

2.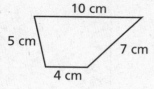

_____

3.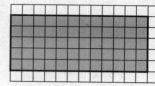

_____

4.

_____

5.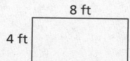

_____

6.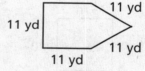

_____

ALGEBRA Find the length of each missing side.

7.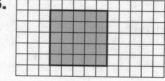

perimeter = 24 in.

_____

8.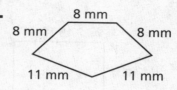

perimeter = 24 ft

_____

9.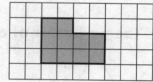

perimeter = 55 yd

_____

Find the perimeter of each item.

10. Gerry plans a rectangular garden plot that is 30 feet long and 15 feet wide. What is the perimeter of the garden plot?

_____

11. A fence around a rectangular corral has a length of 180 feet and a width of 90 feet. What is the perimeter of the fence?

_____

Name _____ Date _____

Reteach

Measure Area

Area is the number of square units needed to cover a region or figure.

You can use these two ways to find the area of a rectangle or square.

- Count the number of square units.
  There are 25 square units.
  The area is 25 square units.

- Multiply the length times the width.
  $5 \times 5 = 25$
  The area is 25 square units.

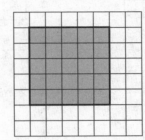

Find the area of each figure.

1.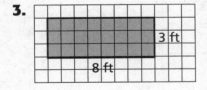

   length: _____ units

   width: _____ units

   area = _____ square units

2.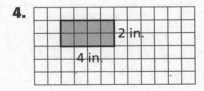

   length: _____ units

   width: _____ units

   area = _____ square units

3.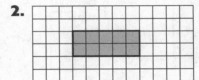

   3 ft

   8 ft

   _____

4.

   2 in.

   4 in.

   _____

5.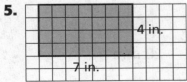

   4 in.

   7 in.

   _____

6.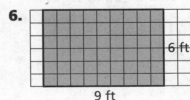

   6 ft

   9 ft

   _____

Name _____ Date _____

Skills Practice

Measure Area

Find the area of each figure.

1.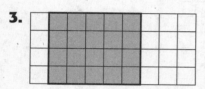

_____

2. 4 ft

4 ft

_____

3.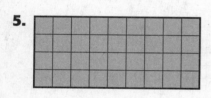

_____

4. 2 in.

2 in.

_____

5.

_____

6. 2 yd

5 yd

_____

**Use grid paper to draw each of the following squares or rectangles.
Tell whether the figure is a *square* or *rectangle*. Then find the area.**

7. length: 5 cm
   width: 8 cm _____

8. length: 7 cm
   width: 7 cm _____

9. length: 7 cm
   width: 4 cm _____

Find the area and perimeter of each figure.

10. 12 cm

    10 cm

11. 1 m [rectangle]
    5 m

12. 7 mm [rectangle]
    28 mm

_____   _____   _____

_____   _____   _____

11-7

Reteach

Problem-Solving Investigation: Choose a Strategy

There are many ways to solve most math problems. You will decide which strategy works best for you when you read the problems.

Problem-Solving Strategies

Act it out: This strategy can help if you have to move things around to see how they fit together.

Guess and check: This strategy can help when there is no pattern and many possible answers.

Look for a pattern: This strategy can help you solve problems when the input changes.

Solve a simpler problem: This strategy can help you break a problem into smaller, simpler problems.

At Sean's school, the Specials teachers rotate which days they come to school. Art is every three days. Music is once a week, rotating days each week. Physical Education is every other day. If he had all three Specials on Monday, which Specials will he have this Friday.

Understand	You know the pattern of his Specials classes. You also know that you need to use the pattern of classes to predict. You need to find out which classes Sean will have on Friday.
Plan	Choose a strategy. There is a pattern for each class. Look at the rule of each pattern. Use the rule to figure out which classes will happen on Friday. Use the look for a pattern strategy to solve the problem.
Solve	The rules are: Art is every three days; Physical Education is every other day; Music is once a week, rotating days.
Check	Check to see if you are correct: Write out which days this week Sean would have Art, Music, and Physical Education. Art: Monday, Thursday Music: Monday Physical Education: Monday, Wednesday, Friday

11–7

Reteach

Problem-Solving Investigation (continued)

Use any strategy shown below to solve. Tell what strategy you used.

- Act it out
- Guess and check
- Look for a pattern
- Solve a simpler problem

1. Steve counted 344 legs at the dog park. If there are 110 guests at the park, how many are people and how many are dogs?

_____

Strategy: _____

2. Arrange these 5 polygons to fit into this shape:

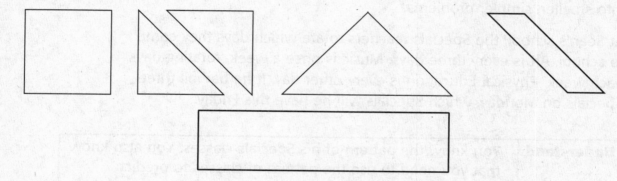

Strategy: _____

3. Sydney earns $1 per square foot that she cleans. If a room were 22 feet by 15 feet, how much would she be paid to clean it? _____

Strategy: _____

4. John can ride his bike 15 miles in 1 hour. Will he be able to complete 100 miles on his bike in 7 hours? _____

Strategy: _____

5. Michael has 88 toy cars. He has 19 more than Javier. Javier has 5 more than Jeff. How many cars does Jeff have? _____

Strategy: _____

11-7

Skills Practice

Problem-Solving Investigation: Choose a Strategy

Use any strategy shown below to solve.
Tell what strategy you used.

- Act it out
- Guess and check
- Look for a pattern
- Solve a simpler problem

1. My brother tells me he has five bills in his wallet and they equal $32. If I can guess which bills they are: $20, $10, $5, $1, he will give them to me. What are the five bills in his wallet?

_____

Strategy: _____

2. Allison cut out this paper to wrap a gift. What shape is the package she will wrap?

_____

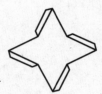

Strategy: _____

3. Elizabeth sells lemonade for $2 a glass after the football games. How much would she earn if she sold 57 glasses at each of four games?

_____

Strategy: _____

_____

4. Eduardo can complete 6 math problems in 15 minutes. Can he can complete 25 problems in one hour?

_____

Strategy: _____

5. Describe the pattern below and provide the next two numbers.

2, 9, 16, 23, _____

Strategy: _____

_____

1-1

Skills Practice

Problem-Solving Investigation: Choose a Strategy

Use any strategy shown below to solve.
Tell what strategy you used.

- Act it out.
- Look for a pattern.
- Guess and check.
- Solve a simpler problem.

1. Mrs. Perth tells me he has lived in two homes and they equal $2,141.00 taxes which he pays. The two are $920.5 to $35.51, he will give it out to me. What are the bills he was paid?

Strategy _____

2. Alison cut out this poster to wrap a gift.
What shape is the poster she will wrap?

Strategy _____

3. Elizabeth sells lemonade for 52¢ a glass.
For the lemonade games, how much would she
earn if she sold 57 glasses at each of four games?

Strategy _____

4. Eduardo can complete 8 math problems in 5 minutes.
Can he complete 24 problems in one hour?

Strategy _____

5. Describe the pattern below, and provide the next two numbers.
2, 9, 16, 23 _____

Strategy _____

Name _____ Date _____

Reteach

Measure Temperature

Temperature is a measure that tells how hot or cold something is. In the same way that there are customary and metric units to measure length, there is a customary and a metric unit to measure temperature.

The thermometer below shows some common temperatures in both degrees Fahrenheit (customary) and degrees Celsius (metric).

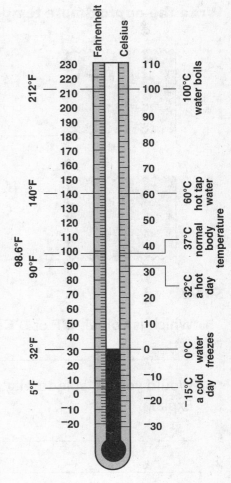

At what temperature does water freeze?

_____

What is 100° C in approximate degrees Fahrenheit?

_____

Write the approximate temperature in degrees Fahrenheit and Celsius. Use the thermometer above.

1. 140°F = _____ °C

2. _____ °C = 100°F

3. 80°C = _____ °F

4. 80°F = _____ °C

5. −15°C = _____ °F

11-8

Skills Practice

Measure Temperature

Write the approximate temperature in degrees Fahrenheit and Celsius.

1.  _____

2.  _____

3.  _____

4. 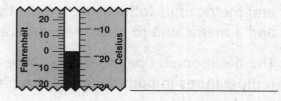 _____

Solve.

5. Which is colder, 0°F or 0°C?

_____

6. Would you be able to play outside if the temperature was 50°C? Explain.

_____

_____

7. A normal human's body temperature is 98.6°F. What is this temperature in degrees Celsius?

_____

Name _____ Date _____

Reteach

Customary Units of Capacity

Capacity is the amount a container can hold. The table lists five customary units of capacity in order from smallest to largest. It also lists a container that is a good estimate for each unit.

Unit	Estimate
fluid ounce	two spoons
cup	cocoa mug
pint	milk carton from school lunch
quart	dog bowl
gallon	large milk jug

Choose the most reasonable estimate for the capacity of an ice cream cone.

A. 1 fluid ounce   **C.** 1 quart

B. 1 cup   **D.** 1 gallon

Look at the chart. Which unit is closest to the capacity of an ice cream cone? _____

An ice cream cone holds more than 1 fluid ounce but less than 1 pint. So, the correct answer is B.

Choose the most reasonable estimate.

1.

A. 8 fluid ounces
B. 8 pints
C. 8 quarts
D. 8 gallons

2.

WATER

F. 1 cup
G. 1 pint
H. 1 quart
J. 1 gallon

1. ____

2. ____

Name _____ Date _____

Skills Practice

Custmary Units of Capacity

Choose the most reasonable estimate.

1.

   A. 1 fluid ounce
   B. 1 cup
   C. 1 pint
   D. 1 gallon

2.

   F. 8 fluid ounces
   G. 8 cups
   H. 8 pints
   J. 8 quarts

   1. ____
   2. ____

3.

   A. 1 gallon
   B. 100 gallons
   C. 1,000 gallons
   D. 10,000 gallons

4.

   F. 1 fluid ounce
   G. 10 fluid ounces
   H. 10 quarts
   J. 100 quarts

   3. ____
   4. ____

5.

   A. 4 fluid ounces
   B. 4 cups
   C. 4 pints
   D. 4 gallons

6.

   F. 1 fluid ounce
   G. 1 cup
   H. 1 quart
   J. 1 gallon

   5. ____
   6. ____

Name _____ Date _____

Reteach

Convert Customary Units of Capacity

You can convert, or change, from one unit of capacity to another. Look at the exercise below. You can use the four-step plan to help you solve this exercise.

7 pt = ▢ c

1 c	= 8 fl oz
2 c	= 1 pt
2 pt	= 1 qt
4 qt	= 1 gal
1 gal	= 128 fl oz

Understand	You must convert 7 pints to cups.
Plan	Are you going from a bigger unit to a smaller unit? If so, multiply. Are you going from a smaller unit to a bigger unit? If so, divide. Pints are bigger than cups, so multiply. There are 2 cups in a pint, so multiply by 2.
Solve	$7 \times 2 = 14$ c There are 14 cups in 7 pints.
Check	To check, convert from cups to pints. $14 \div 2 = 7$ ✓

Select multiplication or division. Then complete each conversion.

1. 48 fl oz = ▢ c

_____

_____

2. 5 gal = ▢ qt

_____

_____

3. 3 qt = ▢ pt

_____

_____

4. 28 qt = ▢ gal

_____

_____

Name _____ Date _____

Skills Practice

Convert Customary Units of Capacity

Complete each conversion.   **Work Space.**

1. 9 pt = ☐ c _____

2. 4 qt = ☐ pt _____

3. 24 fl oz = ☐ c _____

4. 36 qt = ☐ gal _____

5. 10 c = ☐ pt _____

6. 20 pt = ☐ qt _____

7. 6 gal = ☐ qt _____

8. 8 pt = ☐ c _____

9. 17 qt = ☐ pt _____

10. 384 fl oz = ☐ gal _____

Compare. Write >, <, or =.

11. 5 qt ◯ 8 pt _____

12. 8 c ◯ 6 pt _____

13. 20 fl oz ◯ 3 c _____

14. 640 fl oz ◯ 5 gal _____

15. 4 gal ◯ 18 qt _____

16. 9 c ◯ 72 fl oz _____

17. 14 pt ◯ 7 qt _____

18. 12 cup ◯ 4 pt _____

19. 6 qt ◯ 2 pt _____

20. 40 qt ◯ 10 gal _____

Name _____ Date _____

Reteach

Metric Units of Capacity

Two metric units of capacity are the **liter** and the **milliliter**. The table compares these units.

Unit	Abbreviation	Estimate
liter	L	
milliliter	mL	

Look at the cup of water.

Decide whether the cup holds 200 milliliters or 200 liters of water.

The cup cannot hold as much water as the bottle in the chart. It can hold less than 1 liter of water. It cannot hold 200 liters of water. So, 200 milliliters is the more reasonable estimate.

Choose the more reasonable estimate.

1.

250 mL   250 L

_____

2.

4 mL   4 L

_____

Name _____ Date _____

Skills Practice

Metric Units of Capacity

Choose the more reasonable estimate.

1.

   200 mL   200 L

   _____

2.

   100 mL   100 L

   _____

3.

   4 mL   4 L

   _____

4.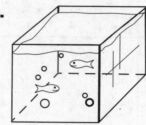

   50 mL   50 L

   _____

5.

   2 mL   2 L

   _____

6.

   175 mL   175 L

   _____

Name _____ Date _____

Reteach

Customary Units of Weight

An object's heaviness is called its **weight**. There are three customary units of weight: ounces, pounds, and tons. The number line below shows the units from lightest to heaviest. It also shows objects that are close estimates for each unit.

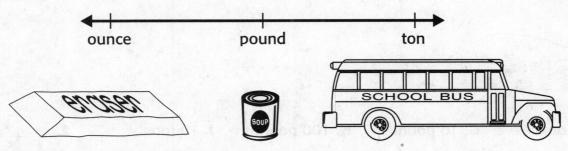

Which is the most reasonable unit measurement for the weight of the computer?

Look at your number line. Where would the computer go on the number line? The computer's weight is more than the soup's weight but less than the bus's weight.

So, pounds are the most reasonable unit.

Choose the most reasonable estimate.

1.

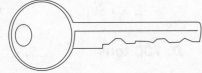

    A. 3 ounces   **B.** 3 pounds   **C.** 30 pounds   **D.** 3 tons   **1.** _____

2.

    F. 1 ounce   **G.** 1 pound   **H.** 1 ton   **J.** 100 tons   **2.** _____

Name _____ Date _____

Skills Practice

Customary Units of Weight

Choose the most reasonable estimate.

1.  red

   A. 2 ounces   **B.** 2 pounds   **C.** 20 pounds   **D.** 2 tons   1. _____

2.

   F. 10 ounces   **G.** 10 pounds   **H.** 100 pounds   **J.** 10 tons   2. _____

3.

   A. 400 ounces   **B.** 40 pounds   **C.** 400 pounds   **D.** 40 tons   3. _____

4.

   F. 15 ounces   **G.** 15 pounds   **H.** 150 pounds   **J.** 15 tons   4. _____

5.

   A. 700 ounces   **B.** 70 pounds   **C.** 700 pounds   **D.** 700 tons   5. _____

6.

   F. 2 ounces   **G.** 2 pounds   **H.** 20 pounds   **J.** 2 tons   6. _____

Name _____ Date _____

Reteach

Problem-Solving Strategy: Use Logical Reasoning

Solve.

Dan needs to put 6 cups of sea salt into the saltwater tank. He has a
7-cup container and a 5-cup container. How can he use the containers
to measure 6 cups?

Step 1. Understand **Be sure you understand the problem.**
Read carefully.

What do you know?

- Dan needs to put _____ cups of sea salt
  in a saltwater tank.

- Dan has containers that hold _____ cups
  and _____ cups.

What do you need to find?

- You need to find how to use the
  containers to measure _____ cups.

Step 2. Plan **Make a plan.**

Choose a strategy.
Use logical reasoning to solve the problem.

You can use the difference in the amount each
container can hold to measure exactly 6 cups.

Step 3. Solve **Carry out your plan.**

Complete the table. It will show how to use
the 7-cup container and the 5-cup container to
measure exactly 6 cups.

Steps	Sea Salt in 7-cup Container	Sea Salt in 5-cup Container	Sea Salt in Tank
1. Fill the 7-cup container.	_____	0	0
2. Fill the 5-cup container from the 7-cup container	_____	5 cups	0

Reteach

Problem-Solving Strategy (continued)

3. Pour what is left in the 7-cup container into the tank.	0	5 cups	_____
4. Repeat steps 1–3. How much sea salt is in the tank now?	0	5 cups	_____
5. Repeat steps 1–3. How much sea salt is in the tank now?	0	5 cups	_____

Step 4. Check   **Is the solution reasonable?**

Reread the problem.

How can you check your answers?

_____

_____

_____

Solve. Use logical reasoning.

1. A worker has a 4-gallon pail and a 9-gallon pail. How can he use them to fill a 10-gallon tank with water?

_____

_____

2. Marcia arrives at the theater 10 minutes before Sam. Sam arrives 25 minutes after Lynn. Paul arrives 10 minutes before Lynn. Lynn gets to the theater at 6:30 p.m. When do the others arrive at the theater?

_____

_____

Name _____ Date _____

Skills Practice

Problem-Solving Strategy: Use Logical Reasoning

Solve.

1. An aquarium worker needs to fill a tank with 10 gallons of water. He has an 8-gallon pail and a 6-gallon pail. How can he use the pails to get exactly 10 gallons of water in the tank?

_____

_____

_____

_____

2. Simon needs to put 9 cups of sea salt into a saltwater tank. He has a 10-cup container and a 7-cup container. How can Simon use the containers to measure 9 cups?

_____

_____

_____

3. The parrot house has 2 times as many birds as the toucan house. The toucan house has 3 more birds than the crane house. The crane house has 6 birds. How many birds do the other houses have?

_____

_____

4. The parrots get food 20 minutes before the toucans. The toucans get food 15 minutes after the cranes. The cranes get food 30 minutes after Bird World opens. Bird World opens at 10:00 A.M. When does each kind of bird get food?

_____

_____

Reteach

Convert Customary Units of Weight

You can convert, or change, from one unit of weight to another. Look at the exercise below. You can use the four-step plan to help you solve this exercise.

16 ounces (oz)   = 1 pound (lb)

2,000 pounds (lb) = 1 ton (T)

Find how many ounces are equal to 6 pounds. 6 lb = ☐ oz

Understand	You must convert 6 pounds to ounces.
Plan	Are you going from a bigger unit to a smaller unit? If so, multiply. Are you going from a smaller unit to a bigger unit? If so, divide. Pounds are bigger than ounces, so multiply. There are 16 ounces in a pound, so multiply by 16.
Solve	$6 \times 16 = 96$ oz There are 96 ounces in 6 pounds
Check	To check, convert from ounces to pounds. $96 \div 16 = 6 \checkmark$

Select multiplication or division. Then complete each conversion.

1. 48 oz = ☐ lb

_____

2. 3 T = ☐ lb

_____

3. 8 lb = ☐ oz

_____

4. 10,000 lb = ☐ T

_____

Name _____ Date _____

Skills Practice

Convert Customary Units of Weight

Complete.   **Work Space**

1. 4 T 500 lb = ☐ lb _____

2. 3 lb = ☐ oz _____

3. 6,000 lb = ☐ T _____

4. ☐ oz = 10 lb _____

5. 64 oz = ☐ lb _____

6. 9 T = ☐ lb _____

7. 3 T 1,000 lb = ☐ lb _____

8. ☐ oz = 4 lb 15 oz _____

9. ☐ T = 12,000 lb _____

10. 2 lb 9 oz = ☐ oz _____

11. ☐ lb = 208 oz _____

12. ☐ lb = 2 T 700 lb _____

13. 144 oz = ☐ lb _____

14. 6 lb 6 oz = ☐ oz _____

15. ☐ T = 16,000 lb _____

Copy and complete the table.

16.

pounds	10	_____	12	_____
ounces	_____	176	_____	208

Name _____ Date _____

Reteach

Metric Units of Mass

Two metric units of mass are the **gram** and the **kilogram**. The table compares these units.

Unit	Abbreviation	Estimate
gram	g	
kilogram	kg	

Look at the watermelon.

Decide whether the watermelon weighs 3 grams or 3 kilograms.

The watermelon weighs more than the paperclip in the chart. It also weighs more than the book, which weighs 1 kilogram. So, the watermelon weighs 3 kilograms.

Choose the more reasonable estimate.

1.

   150 g   150 kg

   _____

2.

   900 g   900 kg

   _____

Name _____ Date _____

Skills Practice

Metric Units of Mass

Choose the more reasonable estimate.

1.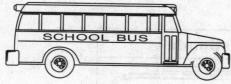

   1,500 g   1,500 kg

   _____

2.

   14 g   14 kg

   _____

3.

   4 g   4 kg

   _____

4.

   45 g   45 kg

   _____

5.

   5 g   5 kg

   _____

6.

   2 g   2 kg

   _____

Name _____ Date _____

Reteach

Estimate and Measure Volume

Volume is the amount of space a solid figure contains. To find an object's volume, count the number of **cubic units** that it contains.

Find the volume of the figure below.

First, count the number of cubic units in the top layer. _____

Next, count how many layers the figure has. _____

Last, multiply the number of cubic units in the top layer by the number

of layers. _____

The volume of the figure is 18 cubic units.

Find each volume.

1.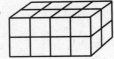

Number of cubic units in top

layer _____

Number of layers _____

Multiplication sentence

_____

Volume _____ cubic units

2.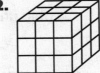

Number of cubic units in top

layer _____

Number of layers _____

Multiplication sentence

_____

Volume _____ cubic units

3.

_____ cubic units

4.

_____ cubic units

Name _____ Date _____

Skills Practice

Estimate and Measure Volume

Find each volume.

1.

   cubic units _____

2.

   cubic units _____

3.

   cubic units _____

4.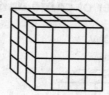

   cubic units _____

5.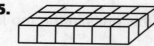

   cubic units _____

6.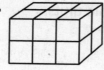

   cubic units _____

Estimate each volume.

7.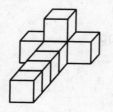

   cubic units _____

8.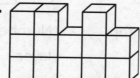

   cubic units _____

9.

   cubic units _____

10.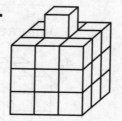

    cubic units _____

Name _____ Date _____

Reteach

Problem-Solving Investigation: Choose a Strategy

To practice for a race, Julia sets up a course using marking tape. She makes tape marks every 3 feet over a distance of 50 yards. The first tape mark is 3 feet from the starting line. How many tape marks does Julia use?

Step 1 Understand   **Be sure you understand the problem.**

Read carefully.

What do you know?

- The tape marks are spread over a distance of _____ yards.

- Julia begins 3 feet from the starting line and places the marks _____ feet apart

What do you know?

- You need to find the number of feet in _____ yards.

- You need to find how many

_____

Step 2 Plan   **Make a plan. Choose a strategy.**

To find the answer, you can draw a diagram.

Find the number of feet in 50 yards.

Show a distance that is that many feet long.

Count by 3s to see how many marks Julia uses if they are placed 3 feet apart.

To find the answer, you can also use logical reasoning.

All the tape marks are the same distance apart.

Use division to find how many marks Julia uses.

Name _____   Date _____

Reteach

Problem-Solving Investigation   (continued)

Step 3 Solve

Carry out your plan.

Read carefully.

How many feet are in 50 yards?
1 yard = 3 feet

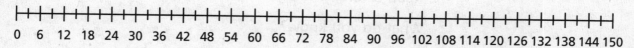

0   6   12   18   24   30   36   42   48   54   60   66   72   78   84   90   96 102 108 114 120 126 132 138 144 150

Draw a diagram. Show a 150-foot distance. Count by 3s, adding tick marks as shown.

Count the tick marks from 3 to 150. Julia uses _____ tape marks.

OR: Use logical reasoning.

The distance is _____ feet. There will be 1 mark every

_____ feet.

Write a division equation. _____ ÷ _____ = _____

Julia uses _____ marks.

Step 4 Check

Is the solution reasonable?
Reread the problem.

Does your answer make sense?   Yes   No
Which method do you prefer? Explain.

_____

Solve.

1. The high school builds 15 rows of stands next to a soccer field. Each row is 30 feet long. How many 10-foot-long boards did they need to build the stands? _____

2. Ed has 4 sets of pictures. There are 24 pictures in each set. He divides the pictures equally among 3 photo albums. How many pictures will each album have? _____

12-9

Skills Practice

Problem-Solving Investigation: Choose a Strategy

Use any strategy shown below to solve. Tell what strategy you used.

- Act it out
- Guess and check
- Look for a pattern
- Solve a simpler problem
- Use logical reasoning

1. The Spirit Club buys 56 yards of material. The material is cut into flags that are 7 feet long. How many flags are made?

_____

2. The Pro Sport Tennis Shop has 156 tennis balls in stock. The tennis balls are packed in tubes of 3. How many tubes of tennis balls does the store have?

_____

3. Larry is building a dog run in his backyard. The dog run is to be 12 feet wide and 30 feet long. If Larry uses sections of fencing that are 6 feet long, how many sections does he use?

_____

4. There are 225 students going to the zoo. Each bus can carry 40 students. How many buses are needed?

_____

5. Tina makes a display of 175 autographed books. She puts 31 books on a large book case. Tina also has 4 smaller book cases. How can she arrange the books on the smaller book cases so that each book case has an equal number of books.

_____

_____

6. Holly uses a pattern to make a display for a grocery store. The first row has 3 peaches, the second row has 6 peaches, the third row has 12, and the fourth row has 24. How many peaches are in the fifth row?

_____

Name _____   Date _____

Reteach

Elapsed Time

Elapsed time is the amount of time that has passed between the start and finish of an activity. You can use the following equation to find elapsed time.

Elapsed time = End time − Start time

Joshua started his homework at 5:15. He finished at 6:30. Find the elapsed time.

Subtract in periods of 15 minutes.

6:30   6:15   6:00   5:45   5:30   5:15

Count the 15-minute periods. _____

Write a multiplication sentence. _____

Simplify. _____

75 minutes, or 1 hour and 15 minutes, of time has elapsed.

The following are the start and end times of activities. How long is each activity?

1.

Count the 15-minute periods. _____

Multiplication sentence _____

Simplify. _____

Elapsed time _____

2.

Count the 15-minute periods. _____

Multiplication sentence _____

Simplify. _____

Elapsed time _____

Name _____ Date _____

Skills Practice

Elapsed Time

The following are the start and end times of activities. How long is each activity?

1.

_____

2.

_____

3.

_____

4.

_____

Find each elapsed time.

5.

What time will it be in

25 minutes? _____

6.

What time will it be in 5 hours and

15 minutes? _____

7.

What time will it be in

10 hours? _____

8.

What time will it be in 6 hours

and 10 minutes? _____

Name _____ Date _____

Reteach

Parts of a Whole

You can use models to show fractions.

This model shows 1.

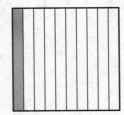

This model shows 1 divided into 10 equal parts. You can shade the model to show $\frac{1}{10}$.

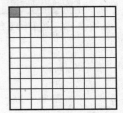

This model shows 1 divided into 100 equal parts. You can shade the model to show $\frac{1}{100}$.

Write the fraction that names part of the whole.

1.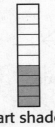

part shaded

_____

2.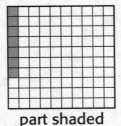

part shaded

_____

3.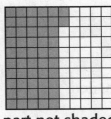

part not shaded

_____

4.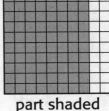

part shaded

_____

Write a fraction for each part identified.

5.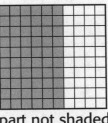

part not shaded

_____

6.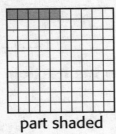

part shaded

_____

7.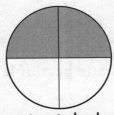

part not shaded

_____

8.

part shaded

_____

13-1

Name _____ Date _____

Skills Practice

Parts of a Whole

Write the fraction that names part of the whole.

1.

part shaded

_____

2.

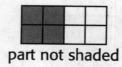
part not shaded

_____

3.

part not shaded

_____

4.

part shaded

_____

5.

part shaded

_____

6.

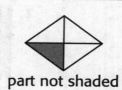
part not shaded

_____

7.

part not shaded

_____

8.

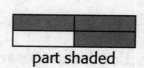
part shaded

_____

Draw a picture and shade part of it to show the fraction.

9. $\frac{1}{3}$

10. $\frac{5}{7}$

11. $\frac{4}{9}$

12. $\frac{4}{5}$

13. $\frac{4}{8}$

14. $\frac{5}{6}$

Grade 4   **242**   *Chapter 13*

Name _____ Date _____

Reteach

Parts of a Set

Pat has three shirts. Two of the shirts are blue and one of them is red.

What you know:

There is a total of **3** things in the set.

One of the 3 things is red.

Two of the 3 things are blue.

To use a fraction to name a part of the whole:

Make the denominator the whole, the total number of things in the set. The numerators are the different parts of the set.

Pat has a total of 3 shirts and 1 of the shirts is red. What fraction of the shirts is red?

$\frac{1}{3}$ or 1 out of 3 shirts is red.

$\frac{2}{3}$ or 2 of the 3 shirts are blue.

_____

Write the fraction for the part of the set that is shaded. Then write the fraction for the part that is *not* shaded.

1. ■ ■ ■ □ □ □ □   2. ▲ ▲ ▲ △   3. ● ● ● ● ○ ○

_____   _____   _____

4. ● ● ● ● ● ○ ○ ○   5. ◆ ◇   6.

_____   _____   _____

Name _____ Date _____

Skills Practice

Parts of a Set

Write the fraction for the part of the set that is shaded. Then write the fraction for the part that is *not* shaded.

1.

2.

_____

3.

_____

4.

_____

5.

_____

6.

_____

Write the fraction that names the part of the set of animals.

7. *not* cats

_____

8. *not* monkeys or rabbits

_____

9. *not* dogs

_____

10. *not* dogs or cats

_____

Solve.

11. Five of 12 students are in the school chorus. What part of the students are in the chorus? _____

12. Twenty of 25 students voted for class president. What part of the class did **not** vote for president? _____

Name _____ Date _____

Reteach

Problem-Solving Strategy: Draw a Picture

Len took a survey among his classmates to find which type of movie they liked best. He surveyed 24 students. He showed his results on a circle graph. How many students chose mystery as their favorite type of movie?

Interpret a Circle Graph

A circle graph shows data as part of a circle. You can interpret the circle graph to solve the problem.

Step 1 What part of this whole chose mystery? What does the circle graph show? The part for Mystery is marked $\frac{1}{6}$.

Step 2 Find the part of 24 students that chose mystery. Rename $\frac{1}{6}$ as a fraction with a denominator of 24.

$$\frac{1}{6} \times \frac{4}{4} = \frac{4}{24}$$

The survey shows that 4 out of 24 students chose mystery.

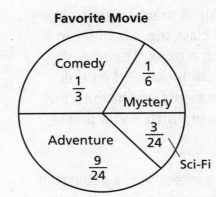

Favorite Movie

Solve. Use the *draw a picture* strategy.

Use the graph to answer these questions.

1. If 20 campers were surveyed about their favorite camp activity, how many chose swimming?

   _____

2. How many chose boating?

   _____

3. How many chose hiking?

   _____

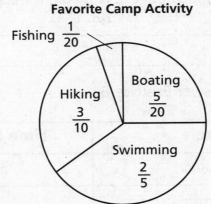

Favorite Camp Activity

13-3

Reteach

Problem-Solving Strategy (continued)

4. **Write About It** Suppose you did not know the number of campers surveyed about their favorite activity. Would you be able to order the activities from most to least favorite? Tell why or why not.

_____

_____

_____

5. There are 15 students in Mr. Black's class. One-fifth of them forgot to bring lunch on the class trip. Six of them forgot to bring a drink. The rest of them have both lunch and a drink. How many students will have to buy either a drink or lunch and a drink?

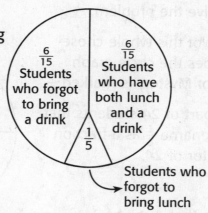

_____

6. There are 12 glasses in the cabinet. If one fourth of the glasses are red, how

many are some other color? _____

7. There are 4 boys. The second oldest is 12. The youngest is 3. The youngest is $\frac{1}{5}$ the age of the oldest. The second oldest is twice the age of the second youngest. How old is each boy?

_____

_____

Use the table to answer Exercise 8.

Name	Time Spent Reading
Joaquin	30 minutes
Benjamin	$\frac{1}{4}$ of an hour
Petrus	$\frac{2}{5}$ of an hour

8. Which of the students spent the most time reading? _____

246

Name _____ Date _____

Skills Practice

Problem-Solving Strategy: Draw a Picture

Solve. Use the *draw a picture* strategy.

1. There are 24 puppies at the pet store. One-third are brown. One-half are black. The rest are some other color, or combination of colors. How many puppies are some other color or combination of colors?

   _____

2. Keanu bought his sister 12 tulips for her graduation. $\frac{1}{3}$ of the tulips were yellow. The rest are red. Which color were there the most of? How many tulips were that color?

   _____

   _____

3. Rosalyn has 24 CDs. One-fourth are classical. One-third are blues. The rest are techno. How many are techno CDs? _____

4. Monica spent $3\frac{1}{2}$ hours swimming in the lake. Cynthia swam in the lake for 190 minutes. Who swam longer? How much longer?

   _____

5. Julia has 3 sizes of fish in her aquarium. The first type of fish is 4 inches long. The second type is $\frac{1}{2}$ as long as the first. The third type is 1 inch longer than the second type. How long are the second and third types of fish?

   _____

6. Write a problem that you can solve by drawing a picture. Solve your problem. Then ask a classmate to solve the problem.

   _____

Name _____ Date _____

Reteach

Equivalent Fractions

Equivalent fractions are fractions that name the same number. To find an equivalent fraction, multiply or divide the numerator and denominator by the same number.

Find fractions equivalent to $\frac{1}{3}$.

$$\frac{1 \times 2}{3 \times 2} = \frac{2}{6} \qquad \frac{1 \times 3}{3 \times 3} = \frac{3}{9} \qquad \frac{1 \times 4}{3 \times 4} = \frac{4}{12}$$

So, $\frac{1}{3}$, $\frac{2}{6}$, $\frac{3}{9}$, and $\frac{4}{12}$ are equivalent fractions.

Find fractions equivalent to $\frac{6}{8}$.

$$\frac{6 \div 2}{8 \div 2} = \frac{3}{4} \qquad \frac{6 \times 2}{8 \times 2} = \frac{12}{16}$$

So, $\frac{6}{8}$, $\frac{3}{4}$, and $\frac{12}{16}$ are equivalent fractions.

Write the fraction for the part that is shaded. Then find an equivalent fraction.

1.

   $\frac{3}{4}$, $\frac{\square}{8}$

2.

   $\frac{3}{6} = \frac{\square}{12}$

3.

   $\frac{2}{10}$, _____

4.

   $\frac{3}{5}$, $\frac{\square}{10}$

5.

   $\frac{4}{8}$, _____

6.

   $\frac{4}{12}$, _____

Name _____ Date _____

Skills Practice

Equivalent Fractions

Write the fraction for the part that is shaded. Then find an equivalent fraction.

1.

   _____

2.

   _____

3.

   _____

Find an equivalent fraction for each fraction.

4. $\dfrac{3}{7} =$ _____

5. $\dfrac{4}{10} =$ _____

6. $\dfrac{3}{21} =$ _____

7. $\dfrac{4}{5} =$ _____

8. $\dfrac{6}{12} =$ _____

9. $\dfrac{10}{30} =$ _____

10. $\dfrac{6}{15} =$ _____

11. $\dfrac{3}{18} =$ _____

12. $\dfrac{5}{15} =$ _____

13. $\dfrac{4}{12} =$ _____

14. $\dfrac{8}{12} =$ _____

15. $\dfrac{9}{24} =$ _____

ALGEBRA Find the value of x.

16. $\dfrac{x}{16} = \dfrac{1}{4}$ _____

17. $\dfrac{1}{5} = \dfrac{10}{x}$ _____

18. $\dfrac{1}{3} = \dfrac{x}{15}$ _____

19. $\dfrac{2}{7} = \dfrac{x}{49}$ _____

Solve.

20. A box contains 6 red pencils and 8 black pencils. What fraction of

    the pencils are red? _____

21. Paul caught 9 bass and 3 trout. What fraction of the fish

    were trout? _____

Name _____ Date _____

Reteach

Compare and Order Fractions

You can use models number lines, and equivalent fractions
to compare and order fractions.

Compare $\frac{2}{3}$ and $\frac{3}{6}$.

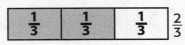

Compare $\frac{3}{4}$ and $\frac{5}{9}$.

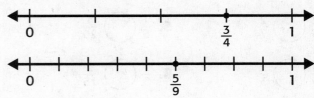

The models show that $\frac{2}{3} > \frac{3}{6}$ and $\frac{3}{4} > \frac{5}{9}$.

To compare three fractions, find equivalent fractions with the same denominator.

$$\frac{3}{4} = \frac{9}{12} \qquad \frac{2}{3} = \frac{8}{12} \qquad \frac{5}{6} = \frac{10}{12}$$

Compare the numerators and order from *least* to *greatest*.

$$\frac{2}{3}, \quad \frac{3}{4}, \quad \frac{5}{6}$$

Compare. Write <, >, or =.

1.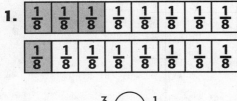

$\frac{3}{8}$ ◯ $\frac{1}{8}$

2.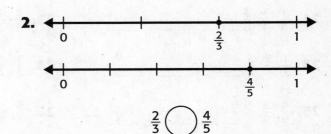

$\frac{2}{3}$ ◯ $\frac{4}{5}$

Order from *least* to *greatest*.

3. $\frac{12}{15}, \frac{1}{3}, \frac{3}{5}$ _____, _____, _____

4. $\frac{5}{8}, \frac{3}{4}, \frac{1}{2}$ _____, _____, _____

5. $\frac{3}{10}, \frac{2}{5}, \frac{1}{4}$ _____, _____, _____

251

Name _____ Date _____

Skills Practice

Compare and Order Fractions

Compare. Write <, >, or =.

1. $\frac{1}{2}$ ◯ $\frac{1}{3}$ 2. $\frac{4}{5}$ ◯ $\frac{12}{15}$ 3. $\frac{7}{12}$ ◯ $\frac{5}{6}$

4. $\frac{2}{5}$ ◯ $\frac{2}{7}$ 5. $\frac{1}{5}$ ◯ $\frac{4}{20}$ 6. $\frac{3}{10}$ ◯ $\frac{4}{9}$

7. $\frac{4}{9}$ ◯ $\frac{2}{3}$ 8. $\frac{1}{5}$ ◯ $\frac{2}{15}$ 9. $\frac{7}{8}$ ◯ $\frac{3}{4}$

10. $\frac{2}{5}$ ◯ $\frac{3}{4}$ 11. $\frac{5}{12}$ ◯ $\frac{1}{4}$ 12. $\frac{9}{10}$ ◯ $\frac{4}{5}$

13. $\frac{7}{10}$ ◯ $\frac{4}{5}$ 14. $\frac{3}{4}$ ◯ $\frac{13}{16}$ 15. $\frac{1}{4}$ ◯ $\frac{5}{16}$

16. $\frac{3}{4}$ ◯ $\frac{2}{3}$ 17. $\frac{8}{9}$ ◯ $\frac{7}{8}$ 18. $\frac{3}{5}$ ◯ $\frac{7}{10}$

Order from *least* to *greatest*.

19. $\frac{1}{4}, \frac{1}{2}, \frac{1}{5}$ ____, ____, ____   20. $\frac{5}{7}, \frac{1}{7}, \frac{4}{21}$ ____, ____, ____

21. $\frac{7}{8}, \frac{3}{4}, \frac{3}{8}$ ____, ____, ____   22. $\frac{4}{9}, \frac{1}{3}, \frac{2}{3}$ ____, ____, ____

23. $\frac{1}{2}, \frac{2}{3}, \frac{3}{4}$ ____, ____, ____   24. $\frac{1}{4}, \frac{3}{4}, \frac{3}{16}$ ____, ____, ____

25. $\frac{4}{9}, \frac{2}{9}, \frac{5}{9}$ ____, ____, ____   26. $\frac{5}{6}, \frac{7}{12}, \frac{3}{4}$ ____, ____, ____

Solve.

27. Sandra eats $\frac{1}{6}$ of a cake. Pat eats $\frac{1}{3}$ of the same cake. Who eats more cake? Explain.

_____

28. Karl eats $\frac{1}{2}$ of a pizza. Tim eats $\frac{2}{3}$ of a pizza. Chris eats $\frac{3}{4}$ of a pizza. Order the amounts from *greatest* to *least*.

_____

13-6

Reteach

Mixed Numbers

A **mixed number** is made up of a whole and a part of a whole.
You can use models to help you write mixed numbers.

Mixed number: $3\frac{1}{4}$
Read: three and one-fourth

An **improper fraction** has a numerator that is greater than or equal to its denominator.

To write a mixed number as an improper fraction, write the mixed number as the sum of the whole number written as a fraction and the part of the whole:

$$3\frac{1}{4} = 3 + \frac{1}{4} = \frac{12}{4} + \frac{1}{4} = \frac{13}{4}$$

Write a mixed number and an improper fraction for each model.

1.
   _____

2.
   _____

Write each as an improper fraction or a mixed number.

3. $\frac{9}{8}$ _____

4. $2\frac{3}{16}$ _____

5. $2\frac{1}{2}$ _____

6. $\frac{47}{3}$ _____

7. $\frac{63}{5}$ _____

8. $1\frac{4}{5}$ _____

9. $5\frac{1}{7}$ _____

10. $7\frac{3}{8}$ _____

Name _____ Date _____

Skills Practice

Mixed Numbers

Write each as an improper fraction or a mixed number.

1. $\frac{9}{7}$ = _____

2. $3\frac{6}{8}$ = _____

3. $6\frac{1}{2}$ = _____

4. $\frac{3}{2}$ = _____

5. $3\frac{1}{5}$ = _____

6. $3\frac{1}{3}$ = _____

7. $\frac{7}{4}$ = _____

8. $1\frac{3}{7}$ = _____

9. $\frac{30}{4}$ = _____

10. $\frac{6}{3}$ = _____

11. $\frac{24}{10}$ = _____

12. $8\frac{3}{4}$ = _____

13. $6\frac{1}{3}$ = _____

14. $\frac{21}{5}$ = _____

15. $\frac{4}{2}$ = _____

Identify each point. Write as a mixed number and an improper fraction.

16.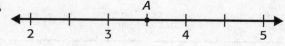

17.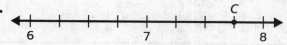

_____

_____

18.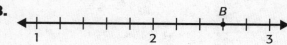

19.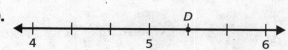

_____

_____

Solve.

20. Adam drinks 11 one-fourths of a cup of milk each day. What is this as a mixed number?

_____

21. John read $\frac{1}{2}$ of his book. Bridget read $\frac{1}{3}$ of her book. Who read more of their book? Explain.

_____

22. Jared drank $\frac{7}{4}$ cups of juice. Aida drank $\frac{9}{6}$ cups. Who drank more juice? Explain.

_____

Reteach

Problem-Solving Investigation: Choose a Strategy

28 students are studying in the library on Thursday afternoon. $\frac{1}{4}$ of them are studying for a history test. 5 students are studying grammar. The rest of the students are studying for a math test. How many students are studying for a math test?

Step 1 Understand	Make sure you understand the problem.
	What do you know?
	There are _____ students. _____ are studying history.
	_____ are studying grammar.
	What do you need to find out?
	_____
	_____
Step 2 Plan • Guess and check • Look for a pattern • Solve a simpler problem • Use logical reasoning • Draw a picture	**Make a plan.** Choose a strategy. You can use logical reasoning to solve.
Step 3 Solve	**Carry out your plan.** Find out the number that equals $\frac{1}{4}$ of 28. $\frac{1}{4}$ of 28 = _____. 7 students are studying history. 5 are studying grammar. $7 + 5 =$ _____ 12 students are studying grammar or history. Subtract 12 from 28. _____ students are studying math.

Name _____ Date _____

Reteach

Problem-Solving Investigation (continued)

Step 4 Check	Is the solution reasonable?
	Reread the problem. Does your answer make sense? Did you answer the question?

Use any strategy shown below to solve. Tell what strategy you used.

- Guess and check
- Look for a pattern
- Solve a simpler problem
- Use logical reasoning
- Draw a picture

1. A group of 18 students goes to the amusement park. Of these students, $\frac{5}{6}$ go on the bumper cars. How many students go on the bumper cars? _____

2. Amiri has 9 cousins. Of these cousins, $\frac{1}{3}$ live in the same town as Amiri. How many of his cousins live someplace else?

_____

3. Angie has $35. She wants to spend three-sevenths of her money on a new pair of jeans. How much money will she have left over?

_____

4. Marge exercises for 45 minutes twice a day. If she keeps up this schedule for 15 days, how many minutes will she exercise in all?

_____

5. Neil has some coins. He has 2 times as many pennies than quarters. He has 4 more nickels than pennies. If he has 4 quarters, how much money does he have? _____

6. Sadie wants to spend 15 minutes every day this week practicing her piano recital piece. Each week until the recital, she wants to double the amount of time she spends playing each day. How many minutes will Sadie spend playing during the entire fourth week?

_____

_____

256

Name _____ Date _____

Skills Practice

Problem-Solving Investigation: Choose a Strategy

Use any strategy shown below to solve. Tell what strategy you used.

- Guess and check
- Look for a pattern
- Solve a simpler problem
- Use logical reasoning
- Draw a picture

Solve.

1. There are 32 rides at an amusement park. Norman goes on $\frac{3}{8}$ of the rides. How many rides does he go on? _____

2. Donna went on 18 rides. If each ride takes 3 ride tokens, and each token costs a quarter, how much did Donna pay for 18 rides?

   _____

3. Ashley puts 45 stamps in an album. She puts the same number of stamps on each page, and 3 stamps on the last page. There are 2 more pages in the album than the number of stamps on each page. How many pages are in the album? How many stamps are on each page? _____

   _____

4. In the 4th grade at Spring Lake School, 189 students have pet cats, 203 students have dogs, and 83 students have cats and dogs. Make a Venn diagram to show this information.

   _____

5. Molly's uncle is cooking a 7-pound beef roast for dinner. It takes 25 minutes per pound to cook. What time should Molly's uncle begin cooking the roast if he wants to serve dinner at 7 P.M.?

   _____

6. Marcus exercises for 45 minutes 4 times a week. During a 10-week period, he had a cold one week and did not get to exercise. How many total minutes did Marcus spend exercising during this 10-week period? _____

Name _____ Date _____

Reteach

Tenths and Hundredths

You can use a model and a place-value chart to read and write decimals. A model and a place-value chart can also help you write a fraction for a decimal.

Using Models

Think: $\frac{5}{10} = \frac{1}{2}$

Using a Place-Value Chart

Ones	Tenths	Hundredths
0	5	

Think: $0.5 = \frac{5}{10} = \frac{1}{2}$

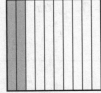

Think: $\frac{60}{100} = \frac{6}{10} = \frac{3}{5}$

Ones	Tenths	Hundredths
0	6	

Think: $0.60 = \frac{60}{100} = \frac{6}{10} = \frac{3}{5}$

**Write a fraction and a decimal for each shaded part.
Then write the fraction in simplest form.**

1.

_____

2.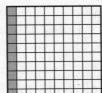

_____

3.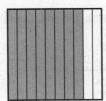

_____

4.

_____

5.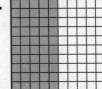

_____

6.

_____

Name _____ Date _____

Skills Practice

Tenths and Hundredths

Write a fraction and a decimal for each shaded part.

1.

2.

3.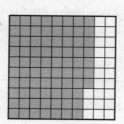

4.

_____ _____ _____ _____

Write each fraction as a decimal.

5. $\frac{2}{5}$ _____

6. $\frac{1}{4}$ _____

7. $\frac{1}{2}$ _____

8. $\frac{2}{100}$ _____

9. $\frac{7}{10}$ _____

10. $\frac{7}{100}$ _____

11. $\frac{1}{10}$ _____

12. $\frac{96}{100}$ _____

13. two tenths _____

14. five tenths _____

15. fifteen hundredths _____

16. seventeen hundredths _____

17. six hundredths _____

18. ninety-nine hundredths _____

19. three tenths _____

20. two tenths _____

Write a fraction and a decimal for each point. Tell if it is closer to 0, $\frac{1}{2}$, or 1.

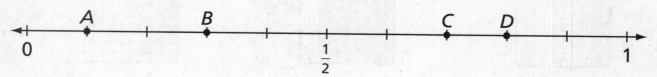

21. A _____

22. C _____

23. B _____

24. D _____

Solve.

25. Peter's house is 0.78 mile from school. Write the number in words.

_____

26. Lora walks for five tenths of an hour. Write the number as a decimal. _____

Name _____ Date _____

Reteach

Relate Mixed Numbers and Decimals

Decimals Greater Than 1

A mixed number is made up of a whole and a part of a whole.
You can use models to help you write mixed numbers as decimals.

Mixed number: $1\frac{7}{10}$
Decimal: 1.7
Read: one and seven tenths

Mixed number: $2\frac{36}{100}$
Decimal: 2.36
Read: two and thirty-six
     hundredths

Write each as a mixed number and decimal.

1.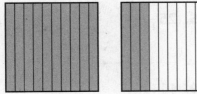

2.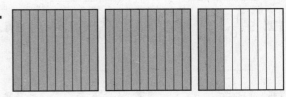

_____   _____

3.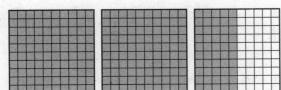

4.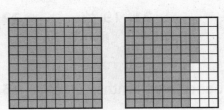

_____   _____

Write each as a decimal.

5. $1\frac{9}{10}$ 6. $3\frac{5}{100}$

_____   _____

Name _____ Date _____

Skills Practice

Relate Mixed Numbers and Decimals

Write each as a mixed number and decimal.

1.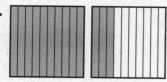

2.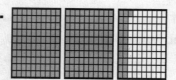

3.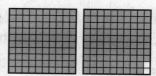

_____   _____   _____

Write each as a decimal.

4. $7\frac{3}{10}$

5. $1\frac{25}{100}$

6. $9\frac{5}{100}$

7. $8\frac{12}{100}$

_____   _____   _____   _____

8. $6\frac{2}{100}$

9. $17\frac{7}{10}$

10. $8\frac{5}{100}$

11. $3\frac{3}{100}$

_____   _____   _____   _____

12. $9\frac{1}{10}$

13. $2\frac{9}{10}$

14. $8\frac{13}{100}$

15. $25\frac{1}{100}$

_____   _____   _____   _____

16. $18\frac{98}{100}$

17. $1\frac{5}{100}$

18. $10\frac{1}{100}$

19. $11\frac{3}{100}$

_____   _____   _____   _____

20. $6\frac{6}{100}$

21. $19\frac{37}{100}$

22. $23\frac{8}{10}$

23. $7\frac{6}{100}$

_____   _____   _____   _____

24. eight and three tenths

25. seven and seventy hundredths

_____   _____

Solve.

26. Out of 100 pairs of shoes in a sporting goods store, 53 pairs are running shoes. What decimal shows the number of pairs of running shoes? _____

27. Out of 100 backpacks, 2 are red and the rest are green, What decimal shows the number of red backpacks?

_____

Name _____ Date _____

Reteach

Problem-Solving Strategy: Make a Model

Alicia baked 24 muffins for her class bake sale. They sell for $1 for 4. How much money will she make for her class?

Step 1 Understand	**Be sure you understand the problem.**
	What do you know?
	• Alicia baked _____ muffins.
	• Muffins sell for _____ for _____.
	• You need to find how much her
	_____

Step 2 Plan	**Make a plan.**
	Make a model by drawing the muffins in groups of 4 with a $1 tag on each group.

Step 3 Solve	**Carry out your plan.**
	Add up the $1 tags for all 6 groups.
	So, 24 muffins will make $6 for the class.

Step 4 Check	**Is the solution reasonable?**
	Reread the problem.
	How can you check your answer? _____

Solve using the *make a model* strategy.

1. Isabel makes and sells pairs of earrings. She uses 5 beads for each earring and charges $0.25 per bead. How much will 10 pairs of earrings sell for? _____

2. There are 2 elephants in a circus act. In their routines, each act uses 2 other animals. How many animals perform altogether?

   _____

3. Mrs. Lee decides to make apple pies. If there are 5 apples in each pie and she makes 4 pies, how many apples will she use altogether?

   _____

Reteach

Problem-Solving Strategy: (continued)

4. Elizabeth has 12 flowerpots. One half of the flowerpots have roses in them. One third of the flowerpots have sunflowers in them. The rest of the flowerpots have daisies in them. How many flowerpots have sunflowers in them? How many flowerpots have daisies in them?

_____

_____

5. Rachel opened 6 packages of paper for her scrapbook. Each package of paper had 20 sheets of blue paper and half as many sheets of green paper. How many total sheets of paper were there?

_____

_____

6. Brianna rollerbladed 2 miles. Then she returned home to get her friend. They rollerbladed together for 3 miles. How far did Brianna go altogether?

_____

7. In the school play, there are 12 props in the first act. There are 33 different props in the second act and 23 different props in the third act. How many different props are there in all?

_____

Name _____ Date _____

Skills Practice

Problem-Solving Strategy: Make a Model

Solve. Use the *make a model strategy*

1. There are 4 jars of fingerpaint in a box. Each child will get 2 jars to use to paint. If there is a class of 16 children, how many boxes of paint will they need?

   _____

2. Ron walked to the store which was 8 blocks away. Then he walked 6 blocks to the park. He had to stop back at the store because he forgot to get something, and then he went home. How many blocks did he walk?

   _____

3. There were 3 cats at the pet shop. The first cat had 6 kittens. The other two cats each had 8 kittens. What was the total number of cats in the pet shop after the kittens were born?

   _____

4. Elena needs to make three dresses. If one dress requires $2\frac{1}{4}$ yards of fabric, how many yards will Elena need for three dresses?

   _____

5. If you have a box of 96 crayons that you want to share with 11 classmates, how many crayons will each classmate receive? Hint: Don't forget to keep crayons for yourself.

   _____

6. Write a problem that can be solved by making a model. Then, ask a classmate to solve the problem.

   _____

   _____

   _____

14-4

Reteach

Locate Fractions and Decimals on a Number Line

Fractions and decimals can be found on number lines. Use the markings between two whole numbers to find a fraction or decimal.

First, find the denominator of the fraction. To do this, count the marks between 5 and 6 on the number line below, including the mark for 6.

There are 4 marks. 4 is the denominator of your fraction.

You can name points on a number line with a letter.

Now find the number that *N* represents. Count the marks between 5 and *N*, including *N*. There are 3 marks. Point *N* is the number $5\frac{3}{4}$. Use what you know to find the decimal. So, *N* is 5.75.

Name each point as a mixed number and a decimal.

1.

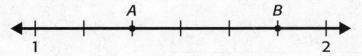

A = _____   B = _____

Name the point *W* represents on each number line as a mixed number and a decimal.

2.

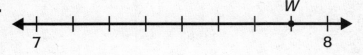

W = _____

3.

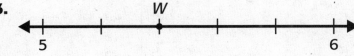

W = _____

Name _____ Date _____

Skills Practice

Locate Fractions and Decimals on a Number Line

Name each point as a mixed number and a decimal.

1.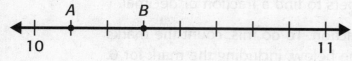

   A = _____   B = _____

2.

   C = _____   D = _____

3.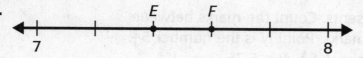

   E = _____   F = _____

4.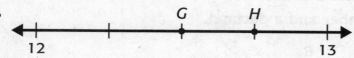

   G = _____   H = _____

Name the point W represents on each number line as a mixed number and a decimal.

5.

   W = _____

6.

   W = _____

Name _____ Date _____

Reteach

Compare and Order Decimals

You can use models to compare and order decimals.
Order the numbers from *least* to *greatest*.

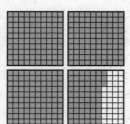

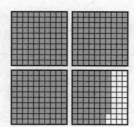

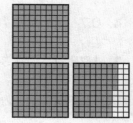

3.63   3.68   2.75

Compare the decimals.	**Order the decimals.**
Since $2 < 3$, $2.75 < 3.63$ and 3.68	Think: $2.75 < 3.63 < 3.68$.
Since $\frac{63}{100} < \frac{68}{100}$, $3.63 < 3.68$.	The order from *least* to *greatest* is 2.75, 3.63, 3.68.

Compare. Write >, <, or =.

1.
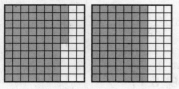

0.75 ◯ 0.7

2.
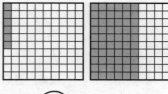

0.06 ◯ 0.60

3.
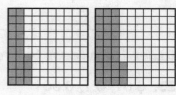

0.24 ◯ 0.33

4.
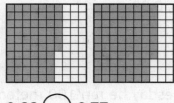

0.66 ◯ 0.77

5.
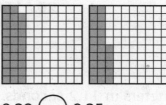

0.29 ◯ 0.25

6.
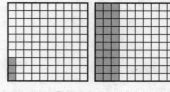

0.03 ◯ 0.30

Order from *greatest* to *least*.

7. 0.75, 0.66, 0.7

8. 0.29, 0.25, 0.24

_____

_____

9. 0.06, 0.77, 0.60

10. 0.33, 0.03, 0.30

_____

_____

Name _____ Date _____

Skills Practice

Compare and Order Decimals

Compare. Write >, <, or =.

1. 0.2 ◯ 0.02   **2.** 11.99 ◯ 12.1   **3.** 16.75 ◯ 16.57

4. 0.7 ◯ 0.70   **5.** 11.1 ◯ 10.1   **6.** 14.44 ◯ 14.54

7. 1.78 ◯ 1.87   **8.** 9.06 ◯ 9.16   **9.** 18.01 ◯ 18.11

10. 12.16 ◯ 12.160   **11.** 6.5 ◯ 5.9   **12.** 9.1 ◯ 9.09

13. 0.106 ◯ 0.160   **14.** 2.1 ◯ 0.2   **15.** 21.12 ◯ 22.13

16. 5.117 ◯ 5.107   **17.** 10.3 ◯ 10.300   **18.** 16.06 ◯ 16.6

Order from *greatest* to *least*.

19. 1.78, 1.08, 1.87   **20.** 1.11, 1.21, 0.22

_____   _____

21. 0.88, 0.08, 0.98   **22.** 10.02, 9.9, 10.12

_____   _____

Order from *least* to *greatest*.

23. 0.01, 0.1, 0.001   **24.** 6.07, 5.99, 6.17

_____   _____

25. 2.22, 2.02, 2.12   **26.** 1.06, 1.16, 0.99

_____   _____

Solve.

27. On Monday Ken ran 100 meters in 11.2 seconds. On Tuesday he ran 100 meters in 10.9 seconds. On which day did Ken run faster?

_____

28. Jadwin Bridge is 1.6 km long. Seely Bridge is 1.06 km long. Which bridge is longer?

_____

Name _____ Date _____

Reteach

Problem-Solving Investigation: Choose a Strategy

Kyle bought birthday balloons for his brother, Jin. Their friends, Steve, Ryan, and Dan, each held one balloon, and Kyle's mom and dad both held 3 balloons. Kyle and Jin had twice as many balloons as their mom and dad. How many balloons did they have altogether?

Step 1 Understand	Be sure you understand the problem.
	What do you know?
	• Kyle bought balloons for his brother.
	• Their 3 friends each held _____ balloon(s).
	• Mom and Dad each held _____ balloons.
	• Kyle and Jin each held _____ balloons.
Step 2 Plan	**Make a plan.**
• Use logical reasoning	Choose a strategy.
• Work a simpler problem	You may draw a picture. Draw each person with the number of balloons they were holding.
• Make a model	
• Draw a picture	
• Look for a pattern	You can also use a four-step plan.
Step 3 Solve	**Carry out your plan.**
	Plan 1 Draw a picture.
	Draw the 7 people at the party with their balloons. Add them up.
	$1 + 1 + 1 + 3 + 3 + 6 + 6 = 21$

Reteach

Problem-Solving Investigation: (continued)

	Plan 2 Use the four step plan. Decide what facts you know. Plan what you will do and in what order. Use your plan to solve the problem. Then check your solution to make sure it makes sense.
Step 4 Check	Is the solution reasonable? Reread the problem. How can you check your answer?

Use any strategy shown below to solve.

- Use logical reasoning
- Work a simpler problem
- Make a model
- Draw a picture
- Look for a pattern

1. Jamie had an aquarium with 8 fish. He had half as many plants, twice as many small rocks, and a quarter the amount of filters. How many plants, rocks, and filters did he have?

   _____

2. Each morning, Joanna jogs with her dog. They jog for 2 miles and walk for 1 mile. How many miles do they walk in 1 week? How many miles do they jog in 10 days?

   _____

3. Julio has 4 cats and 2 dogs. How many total legs do his animals have? How many ears altogether?

   _____

4. Martina ran the 100 M dash in 14.8 seconds and her friend Sandra ran it in 14.2 seconds. Who won?

   _____

14-6

Name _____ Date _____

Skills Practice

Problem-Solving Investigation: Choose a Strategy

Use any strategy shown below to solve.

- Use logical reasoning
- Work a simpler problem
- Make a model
- Draw a picture
- Look for a pattern

1. Carlos had a 55 gallon aquarium with 18 fish. He had half as many plants, twice as many small rocks, and one-sixth the amount of filters. How many plants, rocks, and filters did he have? Estimate how much water each fish had?

_____

2. Each morning, Mario walks his pet dog. They walk for 3 miles. How many miles do they walk in 1 week? How many miles do they walk in 10 days?

_____

3. Joanna has 10 kinds of nail polish. If she uses 2 kinds in a week, how many weeks will it take to use all of them?

_____

4. A building is 45 stories high. Every fifth story is residential and the rest of the building is offices. Laura lives on the third story that is residential. What number will she press on the elevator to go to her home if the ground level is floor 1? _____

5. You saved your money from gifts and allowance and you were able to buy a scooter for $99 and pair of shoes for $24. If you still have $16 left, how much money did you start out with?

_____

6. Ron's mother bought a dozen flowers for $19.99. Alfred's mother bought 2 dozen of the same flowers for $38.98. Whose mother got the better deal?

_____

7. What numbers come next in this pattern? What is the rule? 4, 2, 8, 6, 12, 10, _____, _____, _____.

_____

14-5
Skills Practice
Problem-Solving Investigation: Choose a Strategy

Use any strategy shown below to solve.

Use logical reasoning	Draw a picture
Make a simpler problem	Look for a pattern
Make a table	

1. Carlos has a 55-gallon aquarium with 8 fish. He decided to... many small rocks... and... into the aquarium. How many small rocks... how much water each fish had?

2. ... morning Jenna walks her dog. If they walk for 3 miles, how many miles will they walk in 1 week? How many miles do they walk in 10 days?

3. Tamara has 10 kinds of nail polish. If she uses 1 bottle in 1 week, how many weeks will it take to use all of them?

4. A building is 15 stories high. Every fifth story is residential and the rest of the building is office. Laura lives on the third story that is residential. What number will she press on the elevator to go to her... where the ground level is floor 1? _____

5. You saved money from gifts and allowance and bought were able to buy a radio for $35.00 and a pair of shoes for $25. If you still have $15 left, how much money did you start out with? _____

6. Tom's mother bought a dozen flowers for $19.99. Allied's mother bought 2 dozen of the same flowers for $38.98. Whose mother got the better deal? _____

7. What numbers come next in this pattern? What is the rule? 4, 8, 3, 6, 1, 2, _____

Name _____ Date _____

Reteach

Fraction and Decimal Equivalents

Marsha runs in track and her workout includes a 3.5 mile run and a 0.5 mile cool down. What is the fraction equivalent for Marsha's workout?

Step 1 Understand	**Be sure you understand the problem.**
	What do you know?
	• Marsha runs _____ miles for her workout.
	• Her cool down is _____ miles.
	• You need to find her workout in a
	_____
Step 2 Plan	**Make a plan**
	To find the fraction equivalent to a decimal you can use a number line or model to show the equivalents.
	Write the fraction with a 10 or 100 denominator.
Step 3 Solve	**Carry out your plan.**
	Change the decimals 3.5 and 0.5 to fractions.
	$3\frac{50}{100}$ or $3\frac{5}{10}$ and $\frac{50}{100}$ or $\frac{5}{10}$ or $\frac{1}{2}$
	and  So, $3\frac{1}{2} + \frac{1}{2} = 4$
Step 4 Check	Is the solution reasonable?
	Reread the problem and check your answer.

Write a fraction and decimal to describe the shaded part of each model.

1. ▉▉▉▉▉□□□□□

    _____

    _____

2.

    _____

    _____

Name _____ Date _____

Skills Practice

Fraction and Decimal Equivalents

Write a fraction and decimal to describe the shaded part of each model.

1.

_____

_____

2.

_____

_____

3.

_____

_____

4.

_____

_____

5.

_____

_____

6.

_____

_____

Write each fraction as a decimal.

7. $\frac{36}{100}$

_____

8. $\frac{96}{100}$

_____

9. $\frac{1}{10}$

_____

10. $\frac{3}{10}$

_____

11. $\frac{18}{100}$

_____

12. $\frac{9}{10}$

_____

13. Lauren collects frog figures. She has 4 orange frogs and 21 green ones. Write the proportion of the orange frogs out of the total frogs and the green frogs out of the total frogs as a fraction and a decimal.

_____

_____

Name _____ Date _____

Reteach

Decimals, Fractions, and Mixed Numbers

To compare fractions and decimals, you can write the fractions as decimals and then compare.

You can use a number line to compare fractions and decimals.

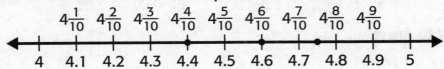

$4\frac{1}{10}$ $4\frac{2}{10}$ $4\frac{3}{10}$ $4\frac{4}{10}$ $4\frac{5}{10}$ $4\frac{6}{10}$ $4\frac{7}{10}$ $4\frac{8}{10}$ $4\frac{9}{10}$

4 4.1 4.2 4.3 4.4 4.5 4.6 4.7 4.8 4.9 5

Place a point on the line where each decimal or fraction belongs. Now you can see whether a decimal or fraction is equal to, greater than, or less than another number.

You can also use a place-value chart to compare numbers: $4\frac{1}{3}$, $4\frac{4}{5}$, 4.6, 4.5.

First, convert fractions to decimals, Example: $4\frac{1}{3} = 4.33$
Line up the decimals points.
Compare the tenths and hundredths place of each number.

Ones	Tenths	Hundredths
4	3	3
4	8	0
4	6	0
4	5	0

From least to greatest: $4\frac{1}{3}$, 4.5, 4.6, $4\frac{4}{5}$.

Compare. Write >, <, or =.

1. 2.5 _____ $2\frac{2}{3}$ **2.** 9.03 _____ 9.3   **3.** $\frac{5}{4}$ _____ $1\frac{1}{4}$

4. $7\frac{7}{8}$ _____ 7.7   **5.** $6\frac{1}{10}$ _____ 6.1   **6.** 13.2 _____ $13\frac{2}{5}$

Order from *greatest* to *least*.

7. $\frac{3}{4}$, 0.5, $\frac{1}{4}$, 0.3 _____

8. $5\frac{2}{5}$, 5.3, 6.0, $5\frac{2}{3}$ _____

9. $10\frac{10}{100}$, 10.15, $10\frac{5}{100}$, 10.0 _____

Name _____ Date _____

Skills Practice

Decimals, Fractions, and Mixed Numbers

Compare. Write >, <, =.

1. $4\frac{4}{100}$ _____ $4\frac{40}{100}$

2. $\frac{4}{5}$ _____ 0.8

3. 6.48 _____ $6\frac{4}{10}$

4. 3.25 _____ $3\frac{1}{4}$

5. 5.35 _____ $5\frac{3}{5}$

6. 0.01 _____ $\frac{1}{10}$

Order from *greatest* to *least*.

7. 0.4, $\frac{6}{100}$, $\frac{1}{5}$, 0.35 _____

8. $25\frac{1}{4}$, 25.5, $25\frac{1}{3}$, $25\frac{1}{7}$ _____

9. $7\frac{7}{10}$, 8.0, 7.65, $7\frac{4}{5}$ _____

ALGEBRA   Use the number line to compare. Write >, <, or =.

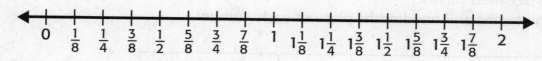

10. $1\frac{1}{6}$ ◯ $1\frac{1}{8}$

11. 1 ◯ $\frac{8}{8}$

12. 2 ◯ $\frac{17}{8}$

Solve.

13. Ben measures $\frac{10}{4}$ cups of water. What is this as a

    mixed number? _____

14. Claudia ran $4\frac{1}{3}$ miles on Monday. On Tuesday she ran $4\frac{1}{2}$ miles.
    On which day did Claudia run a longer distance? Explain.

    _____

15. Jared drank $\frac{7}{4}$ cups of juice. Aida drank $\frac{9}{6}$ cups. Who drank more

    juice? Explain. _____

16. Mary worked $8\frac{1}{2}$ hours on Monday and $8\frac{3}{5}$ hours on Tuesday. On
    which day did she work longer? Explain.

    _____

Name _____ Date _____

Reteach

Round Decimals

You can use a number line to help you round decimals.

To round a decimal to the nearest whole number, look at the digit in the tenths place.
Find the number on the number line.
Round the number to the nearest one.

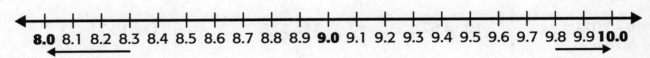

Round 8.3 to the nearest whole number.   Round 9.8 to the nearest whole number.
Think: 8.3 is closer to 8 than 9.   Think: 9.8 is closer to 10 than 9.
So, 8.3 rounds down to 8.   So, 9.8 rounds up to 10.

Round to the nearest whole number.
Use the number line above to help you.

1. 8.6 _____   **2.** 8.2 _____   **3.** 9.8 _____   **4.** 9.6 _____

5. 9.1 _____   **6.** 9.3 _____   **7.** 8.4 _____   **8.** 8.7 _____

To round to the nearest tenth, look at the digit in the hundredths place.
Find the number on the number line.
Round the number to the nearest tenth.

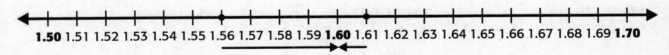

Think: 1.56 is closer to 1.60 than 1.50.   Think: 1.61 is closer to 1.60 than 1.70.
So, 1.56 rounds up to 1.60.   So, 1.61 rounds down to 1.60.

Round to the nearest tenth.
Use the number line above to help you.

9. 1.52 _____   **10.** 1.59 _____   **11.** 1.56 _____   **12.** 1.51 _____

13. 1.64 _____   **14.** 1.63 _____   **15.** 1.68 _____   **16.** 1.66 _____

Name _____ Date _____

Skills Practice
Round Decimals

Round to the nearest whole number.

1. 9.47 _____   2. 1.1 _____   3. 13.61 _____   4. 93.56 _____

5. 2.8 _____   6. 3.51 _____   7. 25.09 _____   8. 88.48 _____

9. 6.01 _____   10. 4.62 _____   11. 37.8 _____   12. 19.71 _____

Round to the nearest tenth.

13. 7.24 _____   14. 1.27 _____   15. 12.57 _____   16. 36.97 _____

17. 9.43 _____   18. 3.98 _____   19. 64.93 _____   20. 53.84 _____

21. 6.58 _____   22. 7.24 _____   23. 47.96 _____   24. 19.46 _____

25. 8.236 _____   26. 3.199 _____   27. 32.333 _____

28. 4.186 _____   29. 17.246 _____   30. 45.999 _____

31. 9.276 _____   32. 26.981 _____   33. 13.462 _____

Solve.

34. A vitamin pill weighs 2.346 grams. What is its mass to the nearest tenth of a gram?

_____

35. Jason weighs 152.6 pounds. What is his weight to the nearest pound?

_____

15-2

Reteach

Estimate Decimal Sums and Differences

To estimate the sums of decimals, round each decimal to the nearest whole number. Then add the rounded numbers.

Estimate 22.62 + 4.49.	Estimate $6.25 − $4.79.
↓ ↓	↓ ↓
Round each number to the nearest whole number. 23 + 4	Round each number to the nearest dollar. $6.00 − $5.00
Add. 23 + 4 = 27	Subtract. $6.00 − $5.00 = $1.00
So 22.62 + 4.49 is about 27.	So $6.25 − $4.79 is about $1.00.

Estimate. Round to the nearest whole number. Show how you rounded.

1. $5.89 + $4.29 _____

2. 17.3 + 5.67 _____

3. 8.48 + 3.07 _____

4. 6.7 + 3.2 _____

5. $15.96 + $2.59 _____

6. 25.7 + 8.9 _____

7. 14.29 − 7.84 _____

8. 10.97 − 7.4 _____

9. 3.62 − 1.87 _____

10. $10.25 − $3.45 _____

11. $10.54 − $7.81 _____

12. 43.7 − 20.48 _____

Name _____ Date _____

Skills Practice

Estimate Decimal Sums and Differences

Estimate. Round to the nearest whole number.

1. $5.1 + 9.4$ _____

2. $7.45 + 8.56$ _____

3. $26.14 - 12.95$ _____

4. $6.7 + 8.4$ _____

5. $4.32 + 7.79$ _____

6. $\$34.95 - \$12.20$ _____

7. $1.9 + 3.8$ ___

8. $8.57 - 3.82$ ___

9. $25.60 - 11.75$ _____

10. $\$6.35 + \$5.95$ _____

11. $17.26 - 13.78$ ___

12. $47.15 - 17.11$ _____

13. $19.76 + 9.95$ _____

14. $77.36 - 15.93$ _____

15. $\$10.25 + \$3.25$ _____

16. $\$16.12 - \$12.80$ _____

17. $19.67 + 9.94$ _____

18. $94.32 - 22.80$ _____

19. $3.7 + 5.2 + 4.6$ _____

20. $\$54.10 - \$34.89$ _____

21. $4.1 + 9.6 + 1.9$ _____

22. $13.4 - 6.79$ _____

23. $2.9 + 6.7 + 7.3$ _____

24. $47.65 - 17.93$ _____

Estimate by rounding to the nearest whole number. Then compare. Use >, <, or =.

25. $3.7 + 2.6$ ◯ $1.9 + 4.2$

26. $7.2 - 4.7$ ◯ $6.8 - 5.8$

27. $4.9 + 1.6$ ◯ $5.1 + 3.1$

28. $5.2 - 2.3$ ◯ $9.7 - 7.9$

29. $7.6 - 2.2$ ◯ $5.6 - 1.3$

30. $7.7 + 7.2$ ◯ $8.1 + 9.1$

31. $8.3 - 6.6$ ◯ $4.2 - 2.3$

32. $8.7 + 9.6$ ◯ $9.1 + 8.6$

33. $5.8 + 6.3$ ◯ $8.2 + 5.2$

34. $1.6 + 2.1$ ◯ $1.7 + 2.0$

Solve.

35. The odometer on a new car shows 17.7 miles. Sean drives the car 12.9 miles. About how many miles does the odometer show now?

_____

36. Nancy ran a total of 5.7 miles today. She ran 3.2 miles this morning. About how many miles did Nancy run this afternoon?

_____

Name _____ Date _____

Reteach

Problem-Solving Strategy: Work Backward

Tim had $5 more yesterday than he does today. Yesterday he had $10.
How much does Tim have today?

Step 1. Understand	**Be sure you understand the problem.**
	 Read carefully.
	
	 • What do you know?
	
	      Tim had _____ more yesterday than he does today.
	
	      Yesterday Tim had _____.
	
	 • What do you need to find?
	
	      You need to find how much _____.

Step 2. Plan	**Make a plan.** Choose a strategy. You can work backward to solve the problem. Start with how much Tim had yesterday. Then work backward to find how much he has today.

Name _____ Date _____

15-3

Reteach

Problem-Solving Strategy (continued)

Step 3. Solve	**Carry out your plan.** You know Tim had _____ yesterday. You know Tim had _____ more yesterday than he does today. Think: Tim had $10 yesterday, which is $5 more than he has today. Subtract to find how much Tim has today. $10 − $5 = $5 Tim has _____ today.
Step 4. Check	**Is the solution reasonable?** Reread the problem. Work forward to check your answer. Start with your answer. Add $5. Did you end with $10? _____ What other strategies could you use to solve the problem? _____

Solve. Use the work backward strategy.

1. Patti had $10 less yesterday than *she* does today. Yesterday she had $1. How much does Patti have today?

   _____

2. Fred and Luis walk to the library. Fred walks twice as far as Luis. Luis walks 2 miles. How far does Fred walk?

   _____

Name _____ Date _____

Skills Practice

Problem-Solving Strategy: Work Backward

Solve. Use the work backward strategy.

1. Carol had $10 less yesterday than she does today. Yesterday she had $15. How much does Carol have today? _____

2. J.R. had 5 baseball cards. Then he bought some more baseball cards at the store. Now J.R. has 9 baseball cards. How many cards did J.R. buy? _____

3. Mr. Robinson and Ms. Alvirez drive to the same movie theater. Mr. Robinson drives twice as far as Ms. Alvirez. Ms. Alvirez drives 15 miles. How far does Mr. Robinson drive? _____

4. Kim has 4 times as many New York quarters as Georgia quarters. She has 24 New York quarters. How many Georgia quarters does Kim have? _____

Solve. Use any strategy.

5. Barry makes letters for a sign that reads "Free Field Trip Sign-Up Sheet." Which letter does Mark need to make the most of?

_____

Strategy: _____

6. Mr. Carlson has $424. He spends $29 on gasoline. How much money does Mr. Carlson have left? _____

Strategy: _____

7. Walking a mile burns about 110 calories. About how many calories would you burn if you walked 2 miles?

_____

Strategy: _____

8. Write a problem that can be solved by working backward. Share it with others.

_____

Name _____ Date _____

Reteach

Add Decimals

You can use models to help you add decimals.

Find 1.34 + 1.28.

Using Models

Color 1.34 dark gray. Color 1.28 with stripes.
Count the number of squares you shaded.

 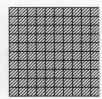

Using Paper and Pencil

Add each place.
Regroup if needed.

```
   1
  1.34
+ 1.28
------
  2.62
```

Add. Use estimation to check for reasonableness.

1. 1.7 + 1.4 = _____

2. 1.24 + 0.38 = _____

3. 0.5 + 0.8 = _____

4. 1.5 + 1.35 = _____

5. 2.25 + 1.03 = _____

6. 1.52 + 0.35 = _____

7. 0.9 + 0.8 = _____

8. 0.6 + 1.85 = _____

9. 0.85 + 0.15 = _____

10. 0.8 + 0.6 = _____

Name _____ Date _____

Skills Practice

Add Decimals

Add. Use estimation to check for reasonableness.

1. 0.36
    + 0.25

2. 0.697
    + 9.262

3. 6.373
    + 5.602

4. 0.29
    + 0.44

5. 23.604
    + 5.408

6. 2.874
    + 8.129

7. 0.60
    + 0.70

8. 32.75
    + 12.30

9. 36.215
    + 9.759

10. 1.67
     + 1.45

11. 25.97
     + 0.12

12. 12.948
     + 7.267

13. 2.67
     + 1.38

14. 12.32
     + 1.74

15. 0.254
     + 12.259

16. 12.5
     + 11.35

17. 2.7
     + 2.73

18. 3.36
     + 5.031

Solve.

19. Lora spends $2.64 on stamps and $1.39 on envelopes. How much does she spend?

_____

20. Ben buys packing tape for $2.97 and boxes for $6.99. How much does he spend?

_____

15-5

Reteach

Problem-Solving Investigation: Choose a Strategy

There are many ways to solve most math problems. You will decide which strategy works best for you when you read the problems.

Problem-Solving Strategies

- Solve a simpler problem
- Make a model
- Use logical reasoning
- Work backward
- Draw a picture

James, Abigail, and Chris each play soccer. James's jersey is not blue. Abigail's jersey is not blue or red. Neither of Chris's two jerseys is green. The color of James's jersey does not begin with r or g. Which color jersey belongs to each of them?

Understand	You know that James has one jersey that is not blue, and the name of the color does not begin with r or g. Abigail has one jersey that is not blue or red. Chris has two jerseys that are not green. You need to find out which color jersey belongs to each person.
Plan	Choose a strategy. You have pieces of information that can help you figure out the correct answer. You will use logical reasoning to figure out the answer.
Solve	Use the pieces of information you have to help you figure out which color jersey each player has. Write yes or no for each piece of information you have. Once you have a yes in a square, you can fill in the rest of the row and column with nos (except for Chris, who has two jerseys):

	red	blue	black	green
James	no	no	yes	no
Abigail	no	no	no	yes
Chris	yes	yes	no	no

Check	Check to see if you are correct: The solution matches the facts given in the problem. So, you know your answer is correct.

Name _____ Date _____

Reteach

Problem-Solving Investigation   (continued)

Use any strategy shown below to solve.
Tell what strategy you used.

- Solve a simpler problem
- Use logical reasoning
- Draw a picture
- Make a model
- Work backward

1. The R train comes every 42 minutes. The next time the R train will arrive is 10:23 A.M. What time did the R train last come?

_____

Strategy: _____

_____

2. The number of acorns on the sidewalk doubles every 6 hours. After 1 day, there are 96 acorns. How many were there at the beginning of the day? _____

Strategy: _____

3. Tim bought 4 books for $16. How much would 15 books cost?

_____

Strategy: _____

4. Two numbers have a product of 48 and a difference of 8. What are these two numbers? _____

Strategy: _____

5. Ashley takes care of her neighbor's pets for $3.50 a day. How many days would she need to work to earn $31.50? _____

Strategy: _____

Name _____ Date _____

Skills Practice

Problem-Solving Investigation: Choose a Strategy

Use any strategy shown below to solve. Tell what strategy you used.

- Solve a simpler problem
- Make a model
- Use logical reasoning
- Work backward
- Draw a picture

1. Kevin's favorite radio station plays his favorite song every 56 minutes. If he heard it at 4:12 P.M., when will the station play the song again? _____

   Strategy: _____

2. Haley spent $6.45 at lunch. Then she repaid her brother $4.27. Now she has $9.18. How much money did she start with?

   _____

   Strategy: _____

3. Tyler bought 3 balls for $10.50. How much would 12 balls cost?

   _____

   Strategy: _____

4. Two numbers have a product of 56 and a difference of 10.

   What are these two numbers? _____
   Strategy:

   _____

5. Hannah and Madison have a leaf collection. Hannah collects three times as many leaves as Madison each day. After 4 days, Madison has 48 leaves. How many leaves per day does Hannah collect?

   _____

   Strategy: _____

6. William, Joe, and Nicole each like running, biking, or swimming. Nicole does not like to wear shoes while exercising. William does not like wearing a helmet. Which sport does each friend like?

   _____

   _____

   Strategy: _____

Name _____ Date _____

Reteach

Subtract Decimals

You can use models to help you subtract decimals.

Find 1.7 − 1.59.

Using Models

Color 1.7. Cross out 1.59.
Count the number of squares not crossed out.

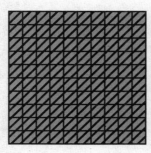 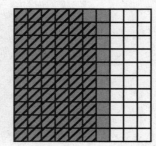

Using Paper and Pencil

Write the numbers. Remember to line up
the decimal points. Subtract each place.
Regroup if necessary.

```
  6 10
  1.70  ←  Write zero as a
− 1.59      place holder.
───────
  0.11
```

Subtract. Check your answers.

1. 1.8 − 1.2 = _____   **2.** 1.35 − 1.08 = _____

3. 0.9 − 0.5 = _____   **4.** 1.7 − 0.48 = _____

5. 1.25 − 0.18 = _____   **6.** 0.5 − 0.05 = _____

7. 0.8 − 0.25 = _____   **8.** 1.65 − 1.3 = _____

Name _____ Date _____

Skills Practice

Subtract Decimals

Subtract. Check your answer.

1. 0.7 – 0.4	**2.** 0.43 – 0.26	**3.** 9.00 – 0.09	**4.** 5.34 – 4.67
5. 6.3 – 0.7	**6.** 0.44 – 0.22	**7.** 7.17 – 2.70	**8.** 1.67 – 0.50
9. 9.1 – 2.3	**10.** 7.04 – 3.66	**11.** 9.04 – 7.50	**12.** 19.83 – 3.60
13. 4.5 – 2.7	**14.** 15.03 – 3.12	**15.** 6.00 – 4.70	**16.** 8.154 – 2.075
17. 1.2 – 0.7	**18.** 4.12 – 1.27	**19.** 8.20 – 4.96	**20.** 17.076 – 0.027

21. 6.7 – 2.4 = _____   **22.** 9.03 – 3.775 = _____

23. 7.6 – 2.07 = _____   **24.** 7.44 – 3.867 = _____

25. 8.5 – 3.08 = _____   **26.** 4.627 – 2.88 = _____

Solve.

27. Christine buys a pair of socks for $8.35. What is her change from a
$10-bill? _____

28. Matt buys a pencil for $0.35, a pen for $2.75, and a ruler for $4.36.
What is his change from a $20-bill? _____